"Ethan Pope is a master of practical and Biblical principles for financial sanity in today's world. After using his MAP program for more than a decade, we have seen God bless our family and ministry tremendously. Following Ethan's counsel has brought us financial stability and blessings that have exceeded our greatest hopes."

DR. CARL MOELLER, *Pastor to Singles Communities*
Saddleback Church, Lake Forest, California

"The most helpful part of Ethan's seminar is the MAP system, which helps families to manage their money wisely. I've never seen anything like it. It is certainly the most workable program I have ever been exposed to!"

ROD MACILVAINE, *Senior Pastor*
Grace Community Church, Bartlesville, Oklahoma

"A mutual friend introduced me to Ethan Pope several years ago when we were preparing to tape a radio show about biblical concepts to guide our financial decisions. I was so impressed that we have called on Ethan many times since then at Moody Broadcasting to help listeners understand sound, biblical principles for managing their money. As a professional, Ethan knows his stuff. Even more importantly, he knows what God's Word says about finances and how to apply godly principles to everyday life."

WAYNE SHEPHERD, *Manager of Programming*
Moody Broadcasting, Chicago, Illinois

"Ethan's simple MAP strategy helped my wife and me break out of a cycle of repeated marital conflict over money and for the first time brought us real financial freedom."

DAVID SCOTT,
Life 2.0, South Bend, Indiana

"As a culture, we long for leaders whose character matches their reputation. Ethan Pope is such a man. Having benefited in a life-changing way from being mentored by Ethan, I wholeheartedly and enthusiastically endorse *Creating Your Personal Money MAP*."

TIM CHASTAIN, *Men's Community Pastor*
Fellowship Bible Church, North Plano, Texas

CREATING YOUR PERSONAL MONEY MAP

Ethan Pope

TYNDALE HOUSE PUBLISHERS, INC.
WHEATON, ILLINOIS

Library of Congress Cataloging-in-Publication Data

Pope, Ethan.
    Creating your personal money map / Ethan Pope.
        p. cm.
Includes bibliographical references.
    ISBN 0-8423-6048-4 (pbk.)
    1. Finance, Personal—Religious aspects—Christianity. I. Title.
HG179.P5577 2004
332.024—dc21   2003013737

Printed in the United States of America

07   06   05   04   03
6   5   4   3   2   1

Acknowledgments and Appreciation

Thank you . . .

to my wife, Janet, who encourages me to always persevere in my writing, speaking, and radio ministry.

to my kids, Natalie and Austin, who continue to bring so much joy to my life. I am so thankful to be your dad!

to my mom, who raised three kids, modeled generosity, carefully managed her money, provided for our needs and practically all our wants, even though money was tight. Thanks, Mom, for a job well done.

to my ministry partners, who are so faithful to pray for our ministry and support it financially. This book is a tribute to your faithfulness and God's provision.

to my friend Dave Bellis for introducing me to Ken Petersen and Tyndale House Publishers. It is an honor to be on the Tyndale team.

to Dave Lindstedt for his expertise as an editor. Your questions, comments, suggestions, and judicious reorganization of content enhanced the clarity and flow of my presentation.

to the thousands of people who have sent letters or e-mails in response to one of my books, seminars, or radio programs. You encourage me to press on every day.

"For not one of us lives for himself, and not one dies for himself; for if we live, we live for the Lord, or if we die, we die for the Lord; therefore whether we live or die, we are the Lord's." (Romans 14:7-8, NASB)

Introduction

AFTER EIGHTEEN YEARS OF TEACHING FINANCIAL SEMINARS, COUNSELING SINGLES and couples, reading thousands of letters, and doing extensive research about Americans and their money, I've come to an inescapable conclusion: The average American family is financially exhausted! Most Americans are stressed out financially, overwhelmed with debt, have little financial discipline, seldom or never plan, support God's kingdom with token gifts, and live literally from paycheck to paycheck. They're on the wrong road, wandering aimlessly through life, with no biblical financial plan. According to surveys I have taken in my seminars, less than 10 percent of the attendees have ever taken the time to create a personal budget and prayerfully evaluate how they give, save, and spend God's resources. How can this be?

In recent years, studies have shown that Americans as a whole have become world-class workaholics who are maxed-out with credit card debt and saving very little of their disposable income. Yet they are always wanting more. Even senior citizens, "once known for their thrift, . . . are piling on debt—filing for bankruptcy in record numbers, and jeopardizing retirement dreams."[1] Some of the side effects of our societal focus on material gain and growth include increases in stress and stress-related diseases, divorce, suicide, homicide, and drug and alcohol abuse.[2] These trends are unlikely to change unless something fundamentally transforms the way we live our lives. Unfortunately, the experience of the average American Christian isn't much different from that of the rest of society. Clearly, this is not God's plan for his people.

Despite the dire outlook, I have good news. Most of our financial problems could be eliminated if individuals and couples would take the time to develop and use a budgeting system that I call a personal money MAP. Sound too simple? It *is* simple and unique, but time and time again since 1985, I have seen that it works. It takes some discipline and determination, but it works.

The Cost of Overspending

One simple reality lies at the root of most financial problems: We spend more than we earn. And, as the following example shows, it doesn't take a lot of overspending to add up to major losses.

If you overspend as little as $2.75 a day (that's less than the cost of the average latte) during the forty-five years of your working life, it could end up costing you $1,233,244.10. The math is very straightforward. If you invested just $82.50 per month ($2.75 per day × 30 days) every month for forty-five years at an 11 percent rate of return, which equals the average annual stock market return over the past fifty years, at the end of that time you would have created an investment account of more than $1.2 million. Even if you earned 6 percent annual return on your investment, you would have $227,369.39. Have you ever considered that God's eternal reward on money invested for his kingdom greatly exceeds 6 or even 11 percent? Could it be that money invested in "good soil" bears fruit thirty, sixty, and a hundredfold? Check it out for yourself in Matthew 13:23.

Please do not read too much into this overused but nonetheless eye-catching financial illustration about overspending $2.75 a day. It may be that spending money on a latte will prove to be one of the best things you do every day. With the MAP, that decision will be up to you! Be assured, however, that the MAP system will *not* train you to walk around with a 3″ × 5″ card tracking every dime you spend. The purpose of the MAP system is to bring *simplicity, gen-*

erosity, consistency, and *freedom* into your financial life—not to drive you insane with details and not to create more millionaires in this world.

As Christians, we should desire to be the best stewards we can be in our giving, saving, and spending. In this book, you will learn proven techniques for how to create and use one of the most basic financial tools: a personal budget. However, for reasons I'll explain, let's not use the word *budget.* Instead, let's call it a *Money Allocation Plan,* or *MAP.* As you'll soon see, this is more than just a matter of semantics. By calling this process a Money Allocation Plan, we focus very deliberately on the choices and decisions that make up a successful money management system. Besides that, everyone can easily understand the concept of using a MAP to get us where we want to go.

I have trained thousands of individuals to use the MAP since it was created in 1985. Used properly, a MAP can alleviate stress, save your marriage, help you to pay all your credit card bills in full every month, accelerate paying off your mortgage, put you on a path to becoming 100 percent debt free, allow you to generously support God's kingdom financially, and help you to be a faithful steward of God's resources. And as I tell my seminar groups, if you're married, the MAP system will help you and your spouse have more fun and less fights!

Sound impossible? Not if you will apply the principles in this book and invest the relatively short amount of time it takes to create your personal MAP. Once you have a MAP in place, all you will need is a half hour to forty minutes each week to remain in control of your financial life and accomplish your goals.

Let me ask you a question: During your twelve to sixteen years (or more) of formal education, how many lessons were you taught on budgeting or money management? If you're like most people, the answer is *zero.* In fact, my conference surveys reveal that less than 10 percent of high school or college graduates have had even one course in personal money management. Isn't that amazing? Our educational system has failed to teach us the first thing about one of the most important aspects of life—something that all of us have to deal with every single day—and that's money. Let's change that right now!

Financially speaking, my desire is to help you find the right road and remain on it for the rest of your life. I am not promising that you will become the next millionaire (nor am I recommending that as a goal), but I am confident that you will be in a better position to live life to its fullest—both financially and spiritually—if you will follow the easy steps of the Money Allocation Plan. For most families, the difference between financial success and failure is determined by how they manage their finances on a daily basis.

Let me encourage you to read this book with an open heart. It could very well be the turning point in your life or marriage. The MAP is a simple tool that will help you move from frustration to freedom, from hurting to healing, from helpless to hopeful, and from foolish to faithful.

Finally, faithful stewards make *daily* decisions with an *eternal* perspective. My prayer for you is that when you come to the end of your life on earth, you'll be able to say with the apostle Paul, "I have fought a good fight, I have finished the race, and I have remained faithful. And now the prize awaits me—the crown of righteousness that the Lord, the righteous Judge, will give me on that great day of his return" (2 Timothy 4:7-8).

Earlier I mentioned the importance of decisions. Now it's decision time. As God's steward, are you ready to implement a simple financial plan that will allow you to be generous in your giving, consistent in your saving, and free in your spending?

If the answer is yes, then let's get started. Together let's create your personal MAP and begin the journey toward spiritual and financial victory in this important area of life called personal money management.

CHAPTER ONE

Which Road Are You On?
Locating Yourself on the MAP

TWENTY YEARS FROM NOW, IF I WERE TO WRITE THE HISTORY OF YOUR family, how would the story unfold? Would it be one of wise decisions and well-earned financial and spiritual rewards, or would it be checkered with foolish financial mistakes year after year? Would your story reflect wise, godly planning and a carefully plotted course, or would it be a tale filled with frustration, defeat, detours, potholes, delays, and failures? From a spiritual perspective, would your life be an example of how to prayerfully and carefully manage 100 percent of the resources God has entrusted to you, or would it be a story characterized by a lack of contentment, wasteful spending, and token giving? Think about it: Will the record show that you were more interested in building your own kingdom or God's kingdom? I urge you not to take these issues lightly. Serious questions demand serious reflection and answers.

I believe that we serve a sovereign God, but in many ways our destiny is in our own hands. The decisions we make today—or don't make—will shape our lives for years to come. They will determine our family legacy and will even affect our eternity. Wise decisions lead to great results. Poor decisions, and sometimes non-decisions, lead to disastrous, often painful results. A lack of adequate *planning* or a lack of good *decisions* or a lack of strong *direction* will all make a difference.

Jesus said, "He who is faithful in a very little thing is faithful also in much; and he who is unrighteous in a very little thing is unrighteous also in much. If therefore you have not been faithful in the use of unrighteous mammon, who will entrust the true riches to you?" (Luke 16:10-11, NASB). If we want God to use us for big things, we must demonstrate faithfulness in the little things, such as managing his resources on a daily basis.

I have spent many years teaching financial seminars, being a guest on live call-in radio programs, and doing personal counseling in the area of finances. Along the way, I have met some couples and individuals who are really enjoying the trip, traveling on a four-lane financial interstate with only occasional bumps or detours. Unfortunately, I've also met others who have taken a wrong turn or two along the way. Those wrong turns, or poor decisions, have led them down dusty, bumpy roads filled with detours, potholes, roadblocks, delays, and daily frustration. Proverbs 13:12 sums up this situation well: "Hope deferred makes the heart sick, but when dreams come true, there is life and joy."

We don't need a huge income to enjoy the trip and avoid most of the financial potholes. We just need to learn how to properly manage the resources that God has entrusted to us.

Teach the wise, and they will be wiser. Teach the righteous, and they will learn more. (Proverbs 9:9)

Fools think they need no advice, but the wise listen to others. (Proverbs 12:15)

If we're wise, we will be teachable, eager to learn what we should or should not do. For example, if we're wise, we will always pay our credit card bills in full every month—and we'll *never* amass huge (or even small) credit card debt that is not paid off. On the other hand, if we're foolish, we will ignore sound advice and wind up living in daily financial bondage due to excessive spending and debt that builds up over the years. The wise person listens to godly counsel—and responds. The fool always has a "better plan," and godly counsel falls on deaf ears.

At my seminars, I can always spot the ones who have been co-erced to attend. Often they will walk into the room with a smirk on their face, sit toward the back with their arms crossed, and never take any notes. Everything about them shouts, "I don't want to be here, and I want you to know that I don't want to be here. I don't like you, I already know what you're going to say, and I dare you to try and teach me anything." The heartbreaking part is that the person's spouse is usually trying to write down every word I say—eager to learn. He or she is desperate for answers and is praying for a miracle.

I usually make a special effort during the break to go and talk to those who came in with a negative attitude. I make it my personal mission to change their minds, primarily out of compassion for their spouse. In most cases, all it takes to break down the barrier is for me to express a genuine interest in them. Before the seminar ends, I might even see them jot an occasional note in their syllabus—but they sure don't want anyone to see them!

Americans and Money

Let's take a closer look at how most Americans view money. As you read, ask yourself how many of these characteristics are true of you.

Optimism

Most Americans are truly optimistic about their financial future. Those of us who were born after the end of World War II grew up in an era of almost unabated economic expansion. As a result, we've come to expect—often without thinking about it—that our financial status will continue to grow. Although this mind-set can be a good thing, in most cases it leads to overspending and other financial problems. We assume we'll be making more money next year than we are now, so we buy a larger home, a more expensive car, and countless other luxuries and "necessities," much of which results in thousands of dollars in credit card debt.

I realize that the "can do" spirit is one of the things that has made America great, but when it comes to overspending, this attitude could lead to our financial destruction. What most Americans really need is more realism, not more positive thinking; more spiritual discernment, not more worldly philosophy. We should all be asking ourselves the question, "How much do I actually have available to live on this year?" rather than "How much might I possibly earn next year?" Optimism is a great attitude, but only if it is grounded in reality.

Stress

The average American family is stressed out. One reason for all the pressure is that we've extended our financial boundaries to the maximum, then gone beyond. I believe that stress is a God-given warning signal. It is not healthy for the body to endure so much stress. In fact, "researchers believe 80 percent of all diseases are linked to or aggravated by chronic stress."[3] It's like pushing the gas pedal to the floor, maxing out the RPMs, and never letting up. Eventually, the engine will blow up and shut down. It's not a question of *if*, only a matter of *when*. Many families live day after day with their financial tachometer in the red zone. Eventually something is going to blow.

The question we should all be asking is this: "What are the things that are causing so much stress in my life, and what am I going to do about it?" For example, if your house payment is taking too much of your income and you never have enough money for food, clothes, and the kids, one option is to *sell the stupid house and move to a less expensive one!* I'm not recommending anything I haven't done myself. In 1988, when Janet and I were living in Richardson, Texas, and beginning our new ministry, finances were very tight. After much prayer, we made one of the hardest decisions we have ever made—we decided to sell our house and (eventually) purchase a house that cost just under half as much as the house we had sold. The good news was that because our larger home had appreciated in value and we had built up some sweat equity over the years, we were able to pay cash for our new home and become 100 percent debt free.

Was it a sacrifice moving into a smaller house? *Without question.* Was it the right thing for us to do? *Without a doubt.* Would we do it again? *Absolutely.*

When we moved from our larger, two-story house into the smaller house, I'm certain we looked like failures to many. But we must learn to make our financial decisions based on God's leadership and what is best for our families, not on what others might think or say about us.

Our decision to move into a smaller house alleviated a major source of stress in our lives. If you're on the road of stress, find a way to make a U-turn before it's too late.

Materialism

Financial burdens and the desire for material possessions have never been greater. Let's face it, Americans are seldom satisfied with their current house, furniture, car, and clothes. If I were to ask you if it is biblically wrong to murder someone, you would say yes. If I were to ask you if it is biblically wrong to commit adultery, you would also say yes. Likewise, if I were to ask you if it is wrong to steal or lie, you would say yes. But what if I asked you if it is biblically wrong to desire another person's house? Before you answer, consider the following scenario:

> Before the new carpet smell wears off, most Americans are looking at the next step up. If they're living in a 1,000-square-foot home, before long they're looking at 1,500-square-foot homes. If they have a 1,500-square-foot home, they can't wait to trade up to a 2,000-square-foot home. But as soon as they obtain the 2,000-square-foot home, a friend buys a 3,000-square-foot home—and the desire to move up begins anew.

Sound familiar? Did you realize that coveting another person's house is on the same list as lying, adultery, and murder? (See Exodus 20:1-17.)

Am I saying that everyone should live in a 1,000-square-foot home? No! Am I saying that it is unspiritual to purchase a larger home? No! Am I saying that God is against large homes? No! What I am saying is that the decision to purchase a larger home should be based upon prayerful consideration of the needs of your family and within the boundaries of your income, not on what your friends and neighbors are doing. The road of materialism and the attitude of never quite being content causes much waste, consumes too much energy, and is spiritually destructive (see Matthew 13:22). If you are traveling in this fast lane, I urge you to get off at the next exit. It's time to find a new MAP.

Debt

Americans are accumulating more and more debt every year. Many are mortgaging their financial future with purchases they cannot afford. Why is this? It boils down to spiritual immaturity and a lack of financial discipline. I'm not saying that all debt equals sin. Let me say that again, just to make sure I'm not misunderstood: All debt does not equal sin! However, many people buy things they really cannot afford and in the long run become slaves to their excessive purchases and debt payments (see Proverbs 22:7). Before we make any purchases, we should ask ourselves two basic questions: "Do I really need this?" and "Can I afford to make this purchase with my present income?" Driving on the dangerous road of excessive debt is like driving at night without any headlights. An accident could happen at any moment. By using a MAP, however, we can unload the debt and turn on the headlights for the rest of the journey.

Marriage and Divorce

Approximately 50 percent of all marriages in the United States end in divorce. Why? In the majority of cases, financial problems are at least a contributing cause. If you are married and looking for a way out, don't choose this exit. The billboards and exit signs all look promising, but once you turn off, you'll find that many of the signs you were reading were simply not true. Most of your problems don't go away when you get a divorce; instead, you just take them with you.

Savings

Americans have never earned more or had more potential for accumulating wealth. However, as a nation we are saving less and less each year. We need to heed the biblical advice in Proverbs 6:6-8 to observe the ant and store up a small surplus. American society is built on consumption. Most Americans live beyond their means, getting by from paycheck to paycheck. If we don't have at least a small surplus, it's like driving without a spare tire in the trunk. We might make it to our destination, but if we get a flat tire, we're in big trouble.

Giving

Most Americans are not givers. In fact, we're pretty stingy when it comes to charitable contributions. With all the freedom and opportunity we enjoy, you'd think we'd be generous and thankful people. But we are so consumed with fulfilling our own self-pleasures that we share only a small token of our resources with others or to support God's kingdom. Many Americans are living selfish lives, but selfishness is a lonely road.

Later in the book we will learn specifically what the Bible says about the importance of giving.

Locating Yourself on the Map

Let's make it personal: How many of these characteristics can you identify with?

- Optimism—Have you been living in the future and not acknowledging the present?

- Stress—Do you need to make changes to remove some of the financial stress in your life?

- Materialism—Do you covet what others have? Are you always looking for bigger, better, or more?

- Debt—Do you purchase things you cannot afford? Does your credit card balance grow every month?

- Marriage and Divorce—Are financial problems causing conflicts in your marriage?

- Savings—Do you have a small surplus for emergencies?

- Giving—Are you a generous giver? What percentage of your income do you give to God's kingdom?

How Are You Doing?

Using the categories above, take a minute right now to locate yourself on the map. Score yourself using a scale from 1 to 10.

1. **Optimism:** Rate your level of optimism from 1 (hard-headed realist) to 10 (unrealistic dreamer). _5_

2. **Stress:** Rate your level of stress from 1 (low stress) to 10 (high stress). _5_

3. **Materialism:** Rate your level of materialism from 1 (always content with what you have) to 10 (never content with what you have). _3_

4. **Debt:** Rate your level of debt from 1 (100 percent debt free, including your mortgage) to 10 (maxed-out, only paying the minimum payment, with some past due bills). _5_

5. **Marriage:** Rate the level of your marriage from 1 (great, wonderful, happy) to 10 (marriage is in serious trouble). _2_

6. **Savings:** Rate your level of savings from 1 (saving at least 10 percent of every paycheck) to 10 (saving nothing). _5_

7. **Giving:** Rate your level of giving from 1 (giving at least 10 percent) to 10 (giving nothing). _1_

What is your total score? _26_

Evaluation Scale

7–14 You are on the financial freeway—almost too good to be true, but I believe you. Maybe you should be writing this book!

15–30 Traveling in the right direction, with occasional detours. You are doing things right—most of the time. You will benefit from using a MAP to eliminate the detours.

31–45 Time for a financial tune-up. You have made some good decisions—and some poor ones. If your score is creeping up into the 40s, you need to be very careful. Use the MAP to regain your direction.

46–60 Traveling a bumpy road. You need a major financial overhaul. Use the MAP to get on the right track.

61–70 You are driving down the financial highway in the wrong direction, with four flat tires, the oil light flashing, no brakes, no lights, running on fumes, and ignoring all the flashing signs and barricades. STOP! Seek financial help immediately, before you crash and hurt yourself and someone else. The MAP can help, but it will require a lot of hard work and discipline to make the necessary changes.

Be honest. Which road are you on—the freeway of wise financial management or the bumpy road of foolish choices and bad decisions? Which direction are you headed—toward biblical stewardship or financial foolishness? How has the trip been so far? Have you encountered numerous detours, complications, and financial frustrations, or has the journey to this point been somewhat pleasant? No matter which track you're on—an eight-lane interstate or a rutted dirt road—I'm convinced that the MAP can help you. Please don't read any further until you have prayerfully taken stock of your personal situation.

CHAPTER TWO

My Personal Financial Journey
Discovering My Need of a MAP

DURING THE EARLY 1980S, I LIVED IN DALLAS, TEXAS, AND WORKED WITH Campus Crusade for Christ and the Josh McDowell Ministry. While I was still single, I purchased a house and lived there for two years with two roommates who were also coworkers. Normally, each evening one of us would stop by the grocery store on the way home from work to pick up some food for dinner, and we would take turns preparing it. When I married Janet, she moved in and the guys moved out. She quickly realized that the refrigerator and pantry were basically empty. We had salt, pepper, and maybe some lemon pepper, but that was the extent of our spices. There was a very limited supply of flour, sugar, and other basics you might expect to find in the pantry.

In her sweet, newlywed voice she said, "Ethan, let's go grocery shopping."

I responded with typical newlywed enthusiasm, "Great, I would love to go with you!"

If you're married, you know that everything you do as a newlywed is exciting—moving into your new apartment or home, going to the bank and ordering new checks, organizing the closet, washing the car, putting the dishes into the dishwasher, buying gas for the car, hanging pictures, painting rooms, wallpapering (okay, maybe not everything), and yes, even going to the grocery store. Before we left the house, I pictured us holding hands as we walked the aisles of the store together, selecting our soft drinks, ground beef, and brownies (which gives you an idea of how I used to eat).

When we arrived at the store, I'm sure I jumped out of the car, ran around to the other side, and opened the door for my new bride. I'm also confident that we walked across the parking lot holding hands. However, as soon as we stepped into the store, everything began to break down—very quickly. First, Janet selected a large grocery cart (which should have been my first clue), and we began going up and down each and every aisle. Eventually, the top part of the cart was full and overflowing, and so was the bottom. By this time, I wasn't holding Janet's hand anymore, because the grocery cart was so full it took both hands to steer it.

Finally, we made it to the checkout counter, and the clerk began to ring up the items. I'll never forget the shock of hearing the total: $169.11. Now remember, this is in 1982 dollars, when $169.11 bought a lot of groceries. If we were to inflate this amount for twenty years at 5 percent, it would be like buying $448.70 worth of groceries—in one trip, for two people. I don't think the checker had ever seen a grown man cry like I did as I wrote out the check.

I don't remember the exact details, but after writing the check I turned to Janet and said something like this: "Janet, I buy groceries by the day, not by the year." Well, as you can imagine, she didn't appreciate that very much. I can assure you we did not leave the grocery store holding hands, and we no doubt went home and discussed it some more. What began as a fun newlywed event ended in a personal financial crisis.

When Two Become One

Before we were married, Janet and I had a great financial relationship. We were never stressed out about money. She had her checkbook and spent money exactly as she pleased. I had my checkbook and spent money exactly as I pleased. It was a perfect relationship. After the wedding, of course, the two checkbooks became one. It was now *our* checkbook. Every time either of us wanted to buy something, we felt an obligation to discuss it with the other person. *We were always talking about money.* It felt like money had become the central focus of our lives.

Finally, Janet came to me and said, "Ethan, I think we need a budget."

"I think you're right," I said. And that was the beginning of our journey toward developing the MAP.

Unfortunately, my initial budgeting plan required a big, three-ring binder with about forty-five different categories and tabs. It was only after using this system for about three years and trying to teach it to others that I realized I had created a useful but somewhat complicated system. The current, one-page MAP system is the result of years of simplification and revision.

As we began to develop the MAP, the first thing we did was determine how much income we expected that year. Then we asked the question, "Where do we need to allocate it?" We started with giving, food, and the mortgage, and we worked our way down through the list. After several hours, we had determined how we would give, save, and spend our money.

We quickly learned that the MAP helped to take the financial stress out of our marriage. Janet realized that if there was money in her Clothing money box when she looked at the MAP form, she could go spend it. No need for us to pray, talk, or fight about it. Actually, if there was money in a MAP category, she had *two* options: She could spend it or leave it in the money box.

I learned that when I looked at the MAP form and saw there was money in my Personal Allowance money box, I could spend it or leave it. No discussion necessary.

Freedom! It was an incredible feeling! The frustration and stress had vanished because we had prayed about our plan when we developed it, and we were now living according to our plan.

However, we also both learned that when we looked at the MAP form and there was no money in one of our money boxes, we had to wait until more was allocated into that specific MAP category before we could spend it. There was no need to pout, cry, stomp our feet, scheme, or even talk about it. No money meant no spending or shopping in that category. Period.

Without a Money Allocation Plan, some families have to discuss *every* spending decision, and this wears them out after a few months or years. If they don't discuss it, they end up fighting over every item purchased—or even worse, one spouse hides a purchase from the other to avoid a confrontation. Several years ago, a woman in tears called my office to ask me if she should tell her husband about the $12,000 in secret credit card bills she had accumulated over the years. I can assure you that secrecy and deception are not a part of God's plan for your marriage. Marriages that last are built on honesty and trust.

I have counseled enough couples over the years to know that most financial problems begin with a breakdown in communication, and they grow one bad decision at a time. But I am convinced that most financial problems can be avoided if individuals and couples will simply take the time to establish a Money Allocation Plan and then follow it.

A MAP will help you live within your means, become debt free, increase your giving, increase your savings, and reduce stress. I encourage you to get out of the rut of living from paycheck to paycheck. I encourage you to change the way you think about and manage money. I invite you to begin living a life that is different from that of the average American and that is honoring to God.

Three Kinds of Money Managers
The Ant, the Sluggard, and the Fake

AFTER YEARS OF TEACHING FINANCIAL SEMINARS, DOING RADIO INTERVIEWS, and providing personal counseling, I have identified three types of money managers, based on descriptions found in the book of Proverbs. My observation is that most people fall into one of these three categories:

- The Ant

- The Sluggard

- The Fake

The diligent, hard-working nature of the ant is legendary, so that category needs little explanation. But let's look at how *Webster's* defines a sluggard and a fake. A sluggard is a "habitually lazy person."[4] A fake is "one that is not what it purports to be . . . a worthless imitation passed off as genuine, [an] imposter [or] charlatan."[5] Fake implies an imitation of or substitution for the genuine but does not necessarily imply dishonesty.

I realize that it's not real flattering to think of ourselves as sluggards or fakes, but I do believe it's important that we take an honest reckoning of how we're managing our finances, and if the shoe fits . . .

Of course, it's always possible to grow and change, but first we must be willing to identify our starting point, including our strengths and weaknesses. To make it easier to compare the three money-management styles, I have summarized the characteristics of the Ant, the Sluggard, and the Fake in the following table, and I have expanded the lifestyle descriptions beyond the actual text.

	ANT	SLUGGARD	FAKE
Key Verse	Proverbs 6:6 (NASB) *Go to the ant, O sluggard, observe her ways and be wise.*	Proverbs 20:4 (NASB) *The sluggard does not plow after the autumn, so he begs during the harvest and has nothing.*	Proverbs 13:7 (NASB) *There is one who pretends to be rich, but has nothing.*
Key Description	Called wise	Does not work	Pretends
Possessions	Possesses riches and honor	Possesses nothing	Has many possessions but an equal amount of debt
Credit Cards	Paid in full every month	Pays the minimum payment or bill is past due	Maxed-out; over-spends and has little discipline in proper use of credit cards; likes to keep and use prestigious cards
Checkbook	Keeps balanced and reconciled	Has no balance; calls bank each day	Orders the most expensive-looking checks to impress people
Home Repairs	Repairs items when broken—many times does self-repair	Will let a broken shutter hang sideways on the house forever	Always calls someone else; time is too valuable for self-repair
Car	Drives a car he/she can afford and keeps it well maintained	Car is always in need of repair due to lack of finances	Usually buys and drives a car he/she cannot afford, but does it to impress others
Home	Buys a home he/she can afford	Probably will never own a home	Always jealous of someone else's home; covets a bigger house

	ANT	SLUGGARD	FAKE
Clothes	Buys clothes as needed; does not waste	Sloppy; does not really care	Must wear popular brand names to impress friends
Goal	Work hard and provide for needs of family	Avoid as much work as possible	Impress people
Problems	Works hard to solve problems	Blames someone else for problems	Tries to hide or cover up problems
Work Ethic	Good	None	Deceptive
Giving	Faithful and generous supporter of God's work	Never has anything to give	Gives money he/she does not really have, only to impress people
Savings	Consistent, steady plodder; has established a small surplus and possibly larger investments	Never saves	Never saves because always has high credit card bills to pay, large mortgage, and expensive car payments
Greatest Need	Not to be prideful or depend on surplus for security	Discipline	Change of self-image
Freedom or Bondage?	Freedom	Bondage	Bondage
Stress Level	Low	High	High
Discipline	High	Low	Low

I'm confident that all of us will find some qualities of the Ant, the Sluggard, and the Fake in our lives. As I look back on the past twenty-five years of my life, there have been times when I would have given myself an A grade, which would represent the wise and hardworking Ant. At other times, I made some stupid decisions that would have earned me an F, which would represent the Fake. And there have been times when I was a little lazy like the Sluggard. But overall, I have tried to live my life according to the example of the Ant: working hard, supporting God's kingdom, providing for the needs of my family, buying only things I can afford, paying my bills, and taking good care of the possessions God has entrusted to me.

Take a few minutes and evaluate your life. Just like me, I'm sure you can remember times when you could identify with the Ant, Sluggard, and Fake. But overall, which model best describes your life now?

The first step in the MAP process is being honest about your present circumstances. If your financial management habits are those of a Sluggard or a Fake, decide right now to take a different approach. One of the greatest things about the Christian life is forgiveness. All of us have made mistakes in the past that we deeply regret. We need to forget what lies behind and press on to the future (see Philippians 3:13-14). Do you feel like you need a fresh start? Do you need to talk with God right now? Do you need to confess your sins and ask God for forgiveness? Read 1 John 1:9 aloud: "But if we confess our sins to him, he is faithful and just to forgive us and to cleanse us from every wrong." God will forgive you if you ask. Have you asked him? If you need to, why not pause right now and do so. If you are married, ask your spouse to join with you in prayer.

With God's help, you can change. Are you still a skeptic about using the MAP? If you don't believe people can change in the area of money management, just read the testimonies of MAP users in the back of this book.

The MAP can help you achieve your goals, but it can't make the decision to change for you. You'll soon discover that if you're not serious about putting into practice the principles found in this book, the MAP system won't work—nor will any other system. But if you desire real financial freedom, you'll find the MAP system life-changing! But first, what does the Bible have to say about money?

CHAPTER FOUR

Budgetology

A Theology of Budgeting

IS BUDGETING BIBLICAL? WHAT DOES THE BIBLE SAY ABOUT MONEY?
How important are our finances to God? When I was a student at Dallas Theological Seminary, my professors gave me numerous opportunities to write special research papers on the topic of stewardship. I devoted hundreds of hours to studying and writing about this area, and I discovered that the Bible contains more than twelve hundred verses dealing specifically with money, possessions, wealth, giving, saving, taxes, debt, contentment, financial setbacks, and greed—just to list a few. If we included the surrounding verses that provide the context in which these specific verses are found, the number of verses referring to financial issues would be upwards of twenty-five hundred to three thousand. In the New Testament, Jesus says more about money and possessions than he does about heaven and hell combined. Any serious Bible student would have to acknowledge that the topic of money and possessions is a major theme in the Bible.

If money is so important to God, can we establish a biblical basis for budgeting? My wholehearted answer is yes! In this chapter, we will examine a theology of budgeting, based on eight foundational principles that will help us to adopt a biblical perspective for our MAP.

1. God Owns Everything

The foundational principle of biblical budgeting is this: God owns everything—100 percent. "The earth is the Lord's, and everything in it. The world and all its people belong to him" (Psalm 24:1). This simple and straightforward truth has profound implications for how we handle money. If everything belongs to God, we would be well advised to consider how he wants us to use what he has given us. Many people mistakenly believe that if they give 10 percent of their income they can do whatever they want with the rest. Nothing could be further from the truth. The money we have is not 10 percent God's and 90 percent ours. It *all* belongs to God. We are merely stewards, or managers, of God's resources. We must understand that we will be held accountable for how we manage 100 percent of the resources entrusted to us by God (see Psalm 24:1; 1 Corinthians 3:8-15; 2 Corinthians 5:10).

Our MAPs take on a new dimension when we realize that we are managing God's money. If we would truly grasp this one concept that God owns everything—I mean, not only understand it intellectually but begin to make all our decisions based on this truth—it would radically change how we give, save, and spend money. God's complete ownership is the single most important principle of Christian stewardship—the bedrock foundation. Everything else we might say about stewardship is based on the truth that God owns it all. If we reject or ignore this basic theology, we have no biblical foundation on which to build. If we neglect this truth, we will be building our financial lives on shifting sand (see Matthew 7:24-27).

Which of the following three options best describes your approach to money?

Option 1: *"I own it all."* This is how most of the world thinks and lives. "I work hard, I earned it, it's mine." People who live according to this philosophy will give only when it serves their own self-interest. More often than not, they'll spend their money on their own pleasures, desires, and interests, often going into debt to "build bigger storehouses" for all their stuff. This financial philosophy has no biblical support. In fact, Jesus calls this kind of person a fool (see Luke 12:13-34).

Option 2: *"I'll give 10 percent to God, but the other 90 percent is mine."* This attitude is very common in the church, and in my opinion it has done great harm to biblical stewardship because it is based on a misunderstanding of Scripture. Those who adopt this philosophy believe that God doesn't care what we do with our money as long as we give 10 percent. But God does care about how we manage all our resources. His desire is that we give at least 10 percent, but he is also interested in how we use the remaining 90 percent.

Could it be that the true test of our stewardship is how we manage what we *keep,* not necessarily just giving our 10 percent? Think about it. It could be that God identifies stewards who are truly trustworthy by how faithfully they allocate the remaining 90 percent of their entrusted resources.

Option 3: *"God owns everything."* This is the only truly biblical perspective. If we acknowledge that everything belongs to God, then we must bring God into our complete financial life, not just what we give. The Christian life is one of wholeness, not compartmentalization. When we compartmentalize, we end up with hidden areas and secrecy. Compartmentalization tempts us to do things that we might want to hide from God and others.

If God owns it all and we are his stewards, then we must bring him into all of our financial decisions. We must prayerfully ask for his guidance on how to allocate all of our resources, whether for giving, housing, transportation, food, clothing, entertainment, spending, saving, and so on.

2. We Are Stewards

It is from the theology of God's ownership that a theology of stewardship is built. A steward is a manager, overseer, or trustee of possessions that belong to another person. Don't miss the pattern of thinking here. As stewards, our allocation of resources should be more "God focused" than "me focused."

Does this mean that in order to be more "God focused" I must give more than I spend on my family for housing, food, clothes, and transportation? No! Here is the issue: Have I prayed about how God desires for me to use 100 percent of the resources he has entrusted to my family? Or do I totally ignore God in making "non-giving" decisions? "Whatever you eat or drink or whatever you do, you must do all for the glory of God" (1 Corinthians 10:31).

REFERENCE	SCRIPTURE
1 Corinthians 4:2	*Now, a person who is put in charge as a manager must be faithful.*
Luke 16:10-12	*Unless you are faithful in small matters, you won't be faithful in large ones. If you cheat even a little, you won't be honest with greater responsibilities. And if you are untrustworthy about worldly wealth, who will trust you with the true riches of heaven? And if you are not faithful with other people's money, why should you be trusted with money of your own?*
Matthew 25:21	*The master was full of praise. 'Well done, my good and faithful servant. You have been faithful in handling this small amount, so now I will give you many more responsibilities. Let's celebrate together!*
Proverbs 28:20 (NASB)	*A faithful man will abound with blessings.*
2 Timothy 2:2 (NASB)	*These entrust to faithful men, who will be able to teach others also.*
2 Timothy 4:7 (NASB)	*I have fought the good fight, I have finished the course, I have kept the faith.*

Figure 4-1

Two Christian families can have a very similar lifestyle (income, house, cars, clothes), but one could be seeking to honor God with their resources while the other has no concept of what it means to be a steward. The Bible says that one will receive a reward in heaven while the other will suffer great loss (see 1 Corinthians 3:10-15 and note the phrases "will receive a reward" and "will suffer great loss"). God entrusts us with resources that we are to use for his honor, which includes meeting the needs of our family, paying for housing and transportation, supporting our local church, supporting other ministries, helping the poor, and being willing to meet special needs.

3. Stewards Are to Be Found Faithful

One of the consistent themes throughout Scripture is the concept of faithfulness. Let's look at just a few examples of what the Bible says about faithfulness (see Figure 4-1). Not every reference specifically refers to the management of money, but each reinforces the principle of our faithfulness to God.

God demands that his stewards be faithful! God honors and blesses faithfulness. God is searching for faithful stewards. "The eyes of the Lord search the whole earth in order to strengthen those whose hearts are fully committed to him" (2 Chronicles 16:9). What is one way we can be faithful? By properly managing God's resources. In practical terms, this means we are not to be careless, wasteful, and foolish with the resources God has entrusted to us.

There is a direct correlation between faithfulness and responsibilities. The more faithfulness we demonstrate in the little things, the more responsibilities we will be given. Why? If God finds us faithful with the resources he has entrusted to us, he might choose to use us as channels of his incredible blessings to others.

4. Stewards Are Conduits for God's Blessings

A conduit is a channel that allows something to flow freely through it without blockage. As stewards of God's resources, we are conduits of his blessings—unless we hoard what we've been given and never pass it along to others. Being a conduit of God's blessings is not always financial. Maybe you know a struggling family that really needs a reliable car. Do you have a car you could give them instead of trading it in on next year's model? Could it be that your demonstration of Christian love will help to bring them to Christ? Do you know a family that has children younger than yours? Do you have some clothing that you could give them? Do you know any single parents who do not have enough money to buy Christmas presents for their kids? Would you be willing to send an anonymous cashier's check? Some of the most blessed times of giving in my life have been the times I gave anonymous gifts.

I know several individuals who made principled decisions to be conduits of God's blessings. They were more interested in sharing their resources than hoarding them or spending them on themselves. Their lives are truly amazing.

The book of Proverbs teaches:

> *It is possible to give freely and become more wealthy,* but those who are stingy will lose everything. The generous prosper and are satisfied; *those who refresh others will themselves be refreshed.* People curse those who hold their grain for higher prices, but they bless the one who sells to them in their time of need. If you search for good, you will find favor; but if you search for evil, it will find you! *Trust in your money and down you go!* But the godly flourish like leaves in spring. Those who bring trouble on their families inherit only the wind. The fool will be a servant to the wise. *The godly are like trees that bear life-giving fruit,* and those who save lives are wise. If *the righteous are rewarded here on earth,* how much more true that the wicked and the sinner will get what they deserve! (Proverbs 11:24-31, emphasis added)

I know a couple who lived on 10 percent of their income one year and gave away 90 percent. Now that is being a conduit of God's blessings! I believe that God built the pipeline and was pumping in the blessings because he knew they were trustworthy stewards. God is searching for other stewards who will be faithful, trustworthy, and generous. Do we all need to be like the family who lived on 10 percent and gave away 90 percent? No. But God does want us to be willing to give freely of our resources.

Stewards come in all shapes and sizes. Some are rich; others are poor. Some are faithful; others are not. Some are very generous; others are greedy. Some seek to honor God with their resources; others seek only to see how much they can honor themselves or spend their resources on selfish pleasures. Some have very little but still desire to be a blessing to others. Even if we are living in poverty, we can be conduits of God's blessings. For example, consider the first-century believers who lived in Macedonia:

> Now I want to tell you, dear brothers and sisters, what God in his kindness has done for the churches in Macedonia. Though they have been going through much trouble and hard times, their wonderful joy and deep poverty have overflowed in rich generosity. For I can testify that they gave not only what they could afford but far more. And they did it of their own free will. They begged us again and again for the gracious privilege of sharing in the gift for the Christians in Jerusalem. (2 Corinthians 8:1-4).

Here's the bottom line from my perspective: Most people, rich or poor, never become conduits of God's blessings because they never develop a biblical basis for stewardship. In God's economy, if we seek first his kingdom, he promises that everything we need (not everything we want) will be ours (see Matthew 6:25-34 and Luke 12:22-30). God gives us resources to use primarily for his glory (see 1 Corinthians 10:31), not for our own. I have yet to find a verse in the Bible that says we're to glorify ourselves. The simple truth is this: It's not about you; it's not about me; it's all about God! We are his stewards, and we must be faithful.

I personally have a lot to learn in this area, but my desire is to become a greater conduit of God's blessings, and I'm convinced that a MAP can help. In order to have the resources to disburse, we must learn how to become wise and prudent with our finances.

5. Becoming Wise and Prudent with Our Finances

Several years ago as I was preparing to speak at a financial seminar, I studied the book of Proverbs, and I became very interested in the concept of developing wisdom and the benefits of being a wise person. My first observation related to how the writer of Proverbs describes the benefits of seeking and having wisdom:

> How blessed is the man who finds wisdom, and the man who gains understanding. For its profit is better than the profit of silver, and its gain than fine gold. She is more precious than jewels; and nothing you desire compares with her. Long life is in her right hand; in her left hand are riches and honor. (Proverbs 3:13-16, NASB)

Is God promising everyone long life and prosperity? No. However, as a general rule, if we exercise wisdom, we are more likely to live longer and have more resources than if we live like fools.

The next passage I studied was Proverbs 8:12 (NASB): "I, wisdom, dwell with prudence." In other words, wisdom and prudence make their home, or reside, together. Therefore, where we find wisdom, we will always find prudence. They are interrelated and interconnected.

What does it mean to be prudent? It is "managing carefully and with economy."[6] Note the progression here. Along with wisdom comes the quality of managing carefully with economy. What does it mean to manage with economy? Economy is the "careful management of wealth, resources; avoidance of waste by careful planning and use; thrift or thrifty use, restrained or efficient use of one's materials; an instance of such management or use as a way of economizing."[7]

Let's connect the dots. Who is blessed? The man who finds wisdom. Where does wisdom dwell? With prudence. What is prudence? Managing carefully with economy. What is economy? Careful management and avoidance of waste. The wise man is prudent, manages with economy, and avoids waste.

I believe that these defining characteristics are a good description of a faithful steward—one who exercises discipline, wisdom, skill, and prudence in the management of God's resources.

6. Wise Stewards Pursue Unity

Stewards should operate with financial oneness in marriage. After all, it's not the husband's money or the wife's money; it's God's money, which he entrusts to the couple to oversee collectively. Financial discord is one of the most common tools Satan will use to try to destroy a marriage. Numerous reports have shown that financial problems are the number one cause of most divorces. If Satan can convince couples to focus on "his and hers," build up walls of division within a marriage, and cause husbands and wives to think more about their own needs than the needs of their spouse and others, he knows they will never have the time or desire to use their resources to honor God.

7. Wise Stewards Are Shrewd Money Managers

In Luke 16:1-13, Jesus tells a story about a dishonest steward who was accused of squandering his master's possessions. When the master called the steward to give an account of his stewardship, the unrighteous steward immediately called in his master's debtors and reduced the amount that each one owed. He was attempting to curry favor with these people so that they would be willing to help him after he was relieved of his stewardship. When the master heard what the unrighteous steward had done, an amazing thing happened: "[The] master praised the unrighteous steward because he had acted shrewdly; for the sons of this age are more shrewd in relation to their own kind than the sons of light" (Luke 16:8, NASB).

How can this be? Why would the master *praise* the dishonest steward? A closer look reveals that the master was not praising his dishonesty but his shrewdness!

In our society, the word *shrewd* sometimes has a negative connotation, implying caginess, deception, or taking advantage of another person. The definition I prefer—and the one that I believe fits the context of Luke 16—is "marked by clever discerning awareness,"[8] which is almost the same as saying "marked by wisdom and prudence." A shrewd steward makes good decisions, wise judgments, and careful expenditures.

If we look at words that are synonymous with *shrewd,* such as *sagacious, perspicacious,* and *astute,* we add to our understanding the ideas of "practical, hardheaded cleverness and judgment," "keen discernment," "unusual power to see what is hidden," "farsighted wisdom," and "diplomatic skill." Don't miss this point: The shrewd steward had the mental capacity to see into the future, plan for his future, and act upon his farsightedness. In this context, Jesus says that "the sons of this age are more shrewd . . . than the sons of light" (Luke 16:8, NASB).

What does all this mean? How can we manage God's resources in a biblically shrewd manner? By understanding the proper use of "unrighteous mammon." Mammon equates to wealth, riches, money, or the currency of this world. In Luke 16, Jesus rebukes the sons of light (believers) for not doing a better job of managing his resources. In practical application, he is challenging us to be shrewder than the "citizens of this world" (those who do not know Christ). If being shrewd in the use of wealth motivates non-Christians, how much more should we who have an eternal perspective be motivated to use our wealth properly? We have far more to gain by using our "worldly resources to benefit others and make friends" (Luke 16:9) than do unbelievers. Our gain is eternal, theirs is temporal, like a vapor (see James 4:13-14, NASB).

As stewards of God's resources, do we have the ability and the farsightedness to see into eternity—that which is obscure, concealed, or veiled—and make decisions based on what we see? Or have we not taken the time to calculate the cost of ignoring what the Bible says about the use of mammon for eternal purposes?

8. Stewards Will Be Held Accountable

Every steward will stand before the Lord and give an accounting of his or her stewardship. "We must all appear before the judgment seat of Christ, that each one may be recompensed for his deeds in the body, according to what he has done, whether good or bad" (2 Corinthians 5:10, NASB). Salvation is not the issue here. Even those who know Christ will give an accounting of their life on earth. Are you being a wise steward of the resources God has entrusted to you? Are you managing with economy and making wise decisions? One day you'll answer for the decisions you make today.

It's never too late to start doing the right thing. We cannot change the past, but I *guarantee* we can change the future. With God's help, we can manage his resources wisely by using a MAP.

As we bring this chapter to a close, I trust you have discovered that budgeting is indeed biblical. So, from a biblical and theological perspective, why should we create a MAP? The answer is logical and straightforward. As we've seen, God owns it all; therefore, we are stewards. As stewards, we are conduits of God's resources and we are called to be wise, prudent, and shrewd managers of those resources. If we know that we will stand before the Lord some day to give an account of our stewardship, it makes sense that we would be motivated to use the best tools we can find to help us manage the resources that God has entrusted to us. My wife and I—and thousands of other people—have discovered that a MAP is a simple and effective tool that *helps* us to be good and faithful stewards.

CHAPTER FIVE

The Big Picture
How the Money Allocation Plan Works

WHEN I WAS GROWING UP, MY FAMILY WENT ON A VACATION EVERY SUMMER. One of my favorite parts was planning the trip and thinking about the exciting places we would visit. As part of the planning, we would lay out a new map of the United States on a card table and highlight the route we would travel during our trip. Before the car ever left the driveway, we knew exactly where we were going and how we were going to get there.

Now that we have a basic understanding of the biblical principles of stewardship, I want to lay the MAP out on the table to guide your trip through the rest of the book. Our goal is to understand the core ingredients that make the MAP work. Once you grasp the big picture, the smaller details will easily fall into place.

Throwing Out the Binder

I taught my first financial management seminar in 1985. I had a great group of eager people in attendance, enthusiasm was sky-high, the room was full of electricity, and everyone left the seminar with high expectations and a big, three-ring binder with about forty-five budget tabs. Looking back on this significant event in the history of our ministry, I can assure you, you would not have wanted to be in attendance at my first financial seminar!

Over the next several weeks, I asked some of the people who had attended the seminar for feedback on what they had learned. Almost without exception, they would tell me,

"Ethan, that was a great seminar. You really did a wonderful job. Thank you for all the time you put into preparing for the seminar."

Then I would ask, "How is the system working for you?" At that point, heads would drop and most would say, "Well, I really have not started using it yet." Not wanting me to feel bad, however, they would add, "But it really is a great system."

It did not take many of these conversations for me to realize that no one—*not even one person*—was using the system. As I look back now, it's no wonder—it was far too complicated! So I tossed my binder with its forty-five sections into the garbage can and went back to the drawing board. I asked God to help me devise a simple system that everyone could and *would* use. As I prayed, I came up with some new guidelines—the seeds of a philosophy of money management that I now call Mapology and a planning tool called the MAP.

You will quickly discover that the MAP approaches budgeting from a unique and fresh perspective. It is not designed to account for how you spend every last dime, but it will help you plan how best to use the material resources God has entrusted to you. If you begin with the right attitude and philosophy—based on the biblical foundation we established in chapters 3 and 4—you will appreciate how the MAP system steers you toward successful money management.

One Piece of Paper—Unfolding the MAP

Here's the big picture: Each month, on one sheet of paper, every dollar from your net (take home) paycheck will be assigned to specific budget categories called *money boxes*. When the time comes to make a purchase, if there is money in the corresponding money box, you can spend it. If the money box is empty, however, you cannot spend any money for one simple reason: It is impossible to take money out of an empty box. The MAP system is based on this simple yet profound truth: You cannot spend what you do not have.

Following the MAP money box system does not mean you will have boxes or envelopes of cash lying around your house. You will deposit your paycheck in the bank, same as usual, but you will allocate every dollar on paper, using a MAP form that includes a series of boxes. This simple form (four sides of a folded 11″ × 17″ sheet of paper) will allow you to create numerous money boxes in which to allocate your resources. I've included a sample MAP form below (Figure 5-1) so you can see what I'm talking about.

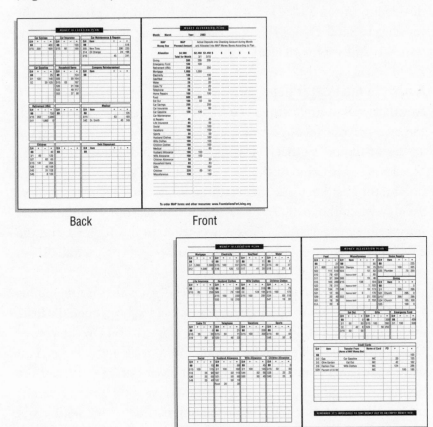

Back   Front

Inside Pages

Figure 5-1

If it looks complicated, fear not! Once I've explained how the whole system works, you'll see just how easy it really is. Here was my logic. I knew that if I could limit the MAP to a single sheet of paper each month (twelve sheets for the entire year), it would have to be a simple system. I was determined not to create anything complex or cumbersome—like a notebook with forty-five tabs that weighs ten pounds!

The first thing I did was to locate the biggest sheet of paper I could find. Taking my inspiration from a road map, I figured it was okay to fold the paper as long as I kept it to one sheet. I finally decided to use an 11″ × 17″ sheet, because by folding it once in the middle, I could create the equivalent of four 8½″ × 11″ pages, which is still very manageable.

A Visit to the Post Office

Another way to understand the Money Allocation Plan is through the eyes of your local postmaster. Have you ever been behind the scenes at the post office? Have you ever wondered what it looks like on the other side of that wall of mailboxes? For every locked box on the customer side there is an open slot on the other side. Every day when the mail arrives, a postal worker allocates the letters into the proper post office boxes according to the addresses on the envelopes. Some mailboxes end up with lots of mail while others receive little or none.

Later, when you go to the post office, you walk into the building, put your key into the lock on your assigned box, open the little door, and look inside. Now here's the point I don't want you to miss: If there is mail in the box, you have a decision to make. You can either leave the mail in the box or take it out. However, if the mailbox is empty, there's no decision to make, because you cannot take mail out of an empty box—it's impossible! If the mailbox is empty, it does absolutely no good for you to stand there and pout, cry, or stomp your feet. No matter what you do or how long you stand there, you cannot take mail out of an empty box.

Your personal MAP operates on the very same principle. Before your paycheck arrives, you will have already assigned every dollar a destination, or money box, based on your prayers, priorities, personal values, plans, and needs. Every time you receive a paycheck, you will allocate the money into the various money boxes, according to your predetermined plan. Then, when you write a check, you are in effect taking money out of a specific money box, just as if you were taking a letter out of your post office box. If there's money in the box, you can spend it; if there's not, you can't.

Allocate Money before It Arrives

One of the keys to a successful Money Allocation Plan is deciding *in advance* how to allocate your paychecks so that every dollar has a predetermined destination. In other words, you will make all your money allocation decisions at the beginning of the month (or year)—before the money ever arrives in your checking account. This is what budgeting or using the MAP is all about—planning ahead instead of relying on spur-of-the-moment decisions about how to spend your money. I'll explain how to do this in a later chapter, but for now just remember the concept.

After every dollar has been allocated, you're free to make individual spending decisions according to your MAP. However, if you do not have a MAP to guide you, it is very easy to make a wrong turn or be led in the wrong direction. In fact, if you don't know where you're going, you could be on the wrong road and not even know it. Wrong turns will sidetrack and delay your financial objectives. Wrong turns waste your time and God's resources and lead to frustration. Too many wrong turns can bring about a financial crisis or destroy your marriage. But it doesn't have to be that way. A personal MAP can keep you on course, moving steadily toward your financial goals. A personal MAP can help you to be a faithful steward of the resources God has entrusted to you.

The MAP can help you set priorities and plan, but the bottom line will always be *discipline*. Having the discipline to follow the system will always be the key to your success. If you will commit yourself and your family to following the MAP, it will be one of the most freeing things you have ever done in your life—*I guarantee it!*

Let me explain to you what makes the MAP so simple and easy to use and why so many people are using it.

Allocating Your Paycheck

To keep things *very simple* at this point, let's start with a Money Allocation Plan with only seven money boxes. (See Figure 5-2 if you prefer a more visual approach.) If your monthly paycheck is $3,000, for purposes of illustration, you might allocate the money as follows:

- $400 into the MAP money box designated for *Giving*.

- $1,000 into the MAP money box designated for *Housing*.

- $600 into the MAP money box designated for *Food*.

- $200 into the MAP money box designated for *Clothing*.

- $400 into the MAP money box designated for *Savings*.

- $300 into the MAP money box designated for *Car Expenses*.

- $100 into the MAP money box designated for *Miscellaneous*.

All these allocations total $3,000, which equals the amount of your paycheck.

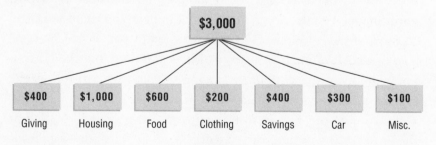

Figure 5-2

Spending Your Paycheck

When you want to make a specific purchase, you would pull out your MAP form, look in the appropriate money box, and if there is money in the money box, you can go ahead and spend it. *Yippee!* You would simply go to the store and write a check for the purchase.[9]

Updating Your MAP

Each week, you would use your checkbook register to update the MAP form. After you have written a check and spent some of the money out of a specific MAP money box, you would remove (subtract) that amount of money from the money box on the MAP form. So, for example, if you went shopping for clothes and spent $200, your MAP money boxes would now look like this:

| $400 | $1,000 | $600 | $0 | $400 | $300 | $100 |
| Giving | Housing | Food | Clothing | Savings | Car | Misc. |

Figure 5-3

When the Money Box Is Empty

Now, what would happen if several days later you saw a pair of shoes on sale and wanted to buy them? The first thing you should do is pull out your MAP form and look in the Clothing money box. Surprise—*the box is empty!* Because the box is empty and because you cannot take money out of an empty box, you cannot buy the shoes until more money has been allocated to that box. There's no use crying or pouting or scheming to get more money to appear, because the MAP merely reflects the plan you made, based on your income and your priorities, before the money even arrived.

There are some occasions when you might move money from one money box to another, but these are rare exceptions, not the general rule. Let me give you one example of a possible exception. Let's say your Car Expenses money box has $300, but you just wrote a check for $400 for a car repair bill. Because it is impossible to take $400 out of a box with only $300 in it, you will need to transfer some money from another source. In this case, you could make the decision to move $100 from your Savings money box into your Car Expenses money box. Remember, this "transfer" takes place on your MAP.

You cannot spend money out of a money box unless sufficient funds are available. This new way of thinking and the discipline it requires might be *really* hard at first, but once you begin to experience the benefits of using a MAP—benefits such as living with less stress and no debt—you will soon become a very committed MAP user. If you have any doubt, just read the MAP user testimonies in chapter 17.

The Big-Picture Approach—No 3″ × 5″ Cards

Here's some more good news: With the MAP system, you won't be carrying around a 3″ × 5″ card to write down every dime you spend. The MAP helps you to focus on the big picture, not on the insignificant details. Every dollar is accounted for, but maybe not in the way you're accustomed to thinking.

The MAP System Looks Forward, Not Back

The MAP is designed to keep you looking forward, not looking back to track where you spent your money. I have met too many people who could tell me to the penny how much they spent on food or clothing this year, but they never use this information to help them make spending decisions today, this week, or this month. All they end up doing is spending hours and hours tracking how they spend their money. In my opinion, tracking is a waste of time. Tracking is simply looking over your shoulder at the past. Really, what good is it if you never use the information to help you make decisions today, tomorrow, or next week?

The primary purpose of the MAP is not to track where the money went but to keep you *on track* according to your plan. Before I go to the grocery store, I should glance at my MAP to see how much I have to spend on food. Before I go to the department store, I should glance at my MAP to see how much I have available in my Clothing money box to spend on clothes. If there's money in the box, I'm free to spend it.

The most important aspect of my system is to train yourself to look at your MAP *before* you spend, not simply to come home after you spend money and record it on the MAP. This mode of operation represents a big difference in how most people use a budget. I don't want to train you to be a "tracker," I want to train you to look at your MAP before you spend any money.

Base Your MAP on Take-Home Pay

The MAP system uses your net income—the total amount of your take-home pay—for one simple reason: It represents the money you have, not the money you don't have. Using your take-home pay instead of your gross income makes it easier to use the MAP. You don't have to worry about accounting for withholding taxes, insurance deductions, pension plans, or any other payroll deductions. This helps to keep the system simple. The less you have to think about, the better.

Because the MAP is based on money you have—your actual take-home pay—you should never fall into the trap that undermines most budgeting systems: spending money you don't have. With the MAP there's no such thing as a negative balance in one of your money boxes. Remember, in the same way that it's impossible to take mail out of an empty mailbox, it is impossible to spend money from an empty money box.

Negative Balances = No Integrity for the System

If you consistently have a zero balance in your Food, Clothing, and Social money boxes, for example, and you cannot correct the problem by adjusting your allocation amounts, but you choose to spend money anyway, there's only one thing left to do: Take your MAP, wad it up, and throw it in the trash can. There's no sense wasting your time updating your MAP if you don't have the discipline to follow it.

Why would I say this? Because if you insist on spending money you don't have out of a specific money box, the MAP has lost its integrity, and it can no longer help you. Likewise, if your Clothing money box says you have $200, but ten other money boxes have negative balances, you really don't have $200 available for clothes. You either need to adjust your allocations or admit that you're just not willing to follow the system. But if you discipline yourself to follow the MAP, overspending is not an option, and you won't have any "negative balance" money boxes.

What if you blow it and do the impossible—take money out of an empty box? Let's look at two scenarios: miscalculation and emergency.

Let's say you forgot to look at your Clothing money box before you went to the mall, and you purchased $125 of clothes. Later, when you are updating your MAP, you're *shocked* to discover that you've done the impossible—you've taken $125 out of a money box that had only $75 in it. An honest mistake, perhaps, but also a good reminder to always look at your MAP *before* you go to the store.

Here's what you do to restore your balance: Simply move money from another money box into the Clothing money box to cover the amount you've overspent. For example, you might move $50 from your Personal Allowance money box or $50 from your Short-Term Savings money box into the Clothing money box to bring the balance up to zero. These kinds of adjustments may be necessary on rare occasions, but don't make this a regular practice or your MAP will become worthless.

Emergency situations are another scenario in which you might overspend your balance in a particular money box, such as Medical Expenses or Car Maintenance. One way to cover this contingency is to transfer money from an Emergency Fund money box or from a Short-Term Savings money box.

Here are three things you *don't* want to do to correct an over-spent balance:

1. Don't "borrow" from next month's allocation. In other words, don't spend money you don't have and then rationalize, "I'll make up for it next month." If you do this, the dam has just developed a small crack and the flood is soon to come. If you start compromising, you'll never stop, and before long your MAP will lack any integrity at all.

2. Don't shrug off spending money you don't have, saying, "Oh, it's no big deal." Being unrealistic will not help you to accomplish your financial goals.

3. Don't decrease your giving to compensate for a lack of discipline in your spending. Get your spending under control. Decreasing your giving will only make your financial situation worse.

Benefits of Using the MAP

The MAP has been around for many years now, and I have seen three common benefits of using the MAP. If you will use the MAP diligently, I believe it will help you become more

- Generous in your giving
- Consistent in your saving
- Free in your spending

Who wouldn't want to enjoy these benefits?

Long-Term Success

I'm convinced that the key to your long-term financial success is

41

how you manage your money on a daily basis—and the best way I've found to manage my own money (the resources God has entrusted to me) is by using a MAP. It may be hard to believe, but using the MAP system reduces stress and may be one of the most freeing things you will ever do.

A close friend of mine told me that before his family started using the MAP, he used to come home from work, look at the checkbook, and get upset about how much money his wife was spending. It didn't matter how much or how little she actually spent. To him it always felt like too much because they didn't have a plan in place to guide them. However, since they have been operating according to the MAP, he no longer gets upset about finances and his wife no longer feels guilty about going to the store. They have a plan, they're sticking to it, their finances are under control, and life has become a lot less stressful.

The Top Ten Benefits of Mapology

Mapology Benefit 1: The MAP operates on one piece of paper each month—no more thick budget notebooks.

Mapology Benefit 2: The MAP is quick and easy to maintain—only thirty to forty minutes per week.

Mapology Benefit 3: Every dollar has an allocation address. You will plan how to give, save, and spend your money ahead of time—before the paycheck arrives and before you're standing in the store looking at all the tempting merchandise.

Mapology Benefit 4: Your MAP will reflect your values, priorities, goals, dreams, and spiritual purpose.

Mapology Benefit 5: You will learn to live within your means because *it's impossible to take money out of an empty box.* You will discover the amazing freedom that comes from discipline and self-control.

Mapology Benefit 6: The MAP takes a "big picture" approach to money management. No tedious tracking of expenditures. No 3″ × 5″ cards. Just look at your MAP before you shop. If there's money in the corresponding money box, you have the option to spend it or let it sit.

Mapology Benefit 7: The MAP looks to the future. Once your Money Allocation Plan is in place, you simply need to follow the system to make it work.

Mapology Benefit 8: The MAP is based on your take-home pay, so you can allocate the money you have, not money you don't have.

Mapology Benefit 9: If you follow the system, the MAP eliminates overspending. There's no such thing as a negative balance in your money boxes. If a specific money box is empty, you don't need to pout, cry, or scheme. You will learn to wait until the next paycheck arrives and additional money is allocated.

Mapology Benefit 10: The MAP allows you to be more generous in your giving, more consistent in your saving, and truly free in your spending.

Once you have experienced the benefits of using a MAP, you will never want to go back to the old way—a life full of stress.

CHAPTER SIX

A Simple Financial Plan
Establishing Your Priorities

SEVERAL YEARS AGO, I WAS PREPARING TO BE A GUEST ON MOODY RADIO'S *Midday Connection,* a live, one-hour, national radio call-in program aired during the noon hour. As I prayed, God kept telling me to offer listeners a *simple* financial plan that would help them establish some biblically based financial priorities. I desired to give them a plan that would be easy to understand, reasonable for most families to accomplish long term, and a plan they could begin working on *today.*

For years, on this program and others, I had been asked repeatedly about priorities: What should I be doing first? Should I pay off my credit cards or put money into my 401(k)? Is it best to pay off my house first or my car? Should I begin investing in mutual funds or pay off my credit card debt first? How much do I need in my emergency fund? Should I support God's kingdom or pay off my debts and then begin to give? The list goes on. . . .

Three Keys for Setting Priorities

In order for the MAP system to work, we need three important elements to be at the center of the process:

> 1. Direction: We need to know where we are starting financially and where we want to go. And as we discussed in chapter 3, we need to understand biblical stewardship and God's priorities for the resources he has placed in our hands.

2. Planning: We need to establish priorities and allocate every dollar from our paychecks.

3. Commitment: We need to commit ourselves to following the MAP. Commitment is the catalyst that makes the engine run smoothly.

I believe that you will find my simple financial plan helpful as you create your MAP. It will help you establish some "big picture" priorities for properly allocating the resources God has entrusted to you. My plan does not cover every aspect of financial planning (such as the need for basic insurance coverage or estate planning), but if you have nothing in place right now, it is a great start.

Priority 1: Elevate Your Giving

At the very core of our simple financial plan, from a biblical perspective, is a commitment to give at least 10 percent of our income to support God's kingdom (see Malachi 3:8-10). Let me say that again, with a slightly different emphasis: Your highest financial priority should be to give *at least* 10 percent of your income. Without a commitment to give, you will never be able to live fully in God's economy.

Giving is what we should do first—not last—with our money. This is what the Bible refers to as giving of our firstfruits. "Honor the Lord with your wealth, with the firstfruits of all your crops; then your barns will be filled to overflowing, and your vats will brim over with new wine" (Proverbs 3:9-10, NIV). We're to give to God first, not from what is left over at the end of the month after we have spent most of it. The world teaches us to "pay yourself first." There is a time to save, but from a biblical perspective, it is not your first priority. The Bible clearly teaches that giving should be our first priority.

Let me be very specific. You should give first even when you're in debt. Give first even if you have to sacrifice new clothes or eating out. Give first even if you have to cut off cable TV or your Internet service. Are you living in need and never seem to have enough?

Does it seem as if you are earning money only to put it into a pocket with holes in it? If this is true of you, the Bible says that you should seriously consider your ways and stop neglecting to give God your best (see Malachi 1:6-10 and Haggai 1:3-7).

When you establish giving as your highest financial priority, you demonstrate by your actions that God really does own it all, that you are a steward who desires to be faithful, and that you trust God to provide for your needs. It is on this foundation that you will build the rest of your plan.

I am often asked, "Should I give based on my gross or net [take-home] income?" My answer has always been, "Do you want God to bless you based on your gross or net income?" Here's what the apostle Paul says about giving in 2 Corinthians 9:6-8:

> Remember this—a farmer who plants only a few seeds will get a small crop. But the one who plants generously will get a generous crop. You must each make up your own mind as to how much you should give. Don't give reluctantly or in response to pressure. For God loves the person who gives cheerfully. And God will generously provide all you need. Then you will always have everything you need and plenty left over to share with others.

Key Point: Here's a practical suggestion to help you consciously make giving your top priority: After your paycheck has been deposited and you have updated your MAP, why not make the first check (or checks) you write be for giving to the Lord's work? In a very tangible way, you will be giving of your firstfruits, thereby demonstrating your faith in God and acknowledging that he is first in your life.

Priority 2: Establish an Emergency Fund

After you are faithfully giving at least 10 percent of your income to God's kingdom, your next immediate priority will be to establish an emergency fund of $500 or 3 percent of your annual take-home pay, whichever is greater. So, for example, if your annual income is $17,000 or less, you would allocate $500 to your emergency fund. If your annual take-home pay is $50,000, you would allocate $1,500 ($50,000 x .03 = $1,500). This allocation is simply to create a minimum emergency fund. Once you have established other immediate priorities, you will work to expand your emergency fund (see Priority 5 below).

If you do not have at least the minimum amount allocated into an Emergency Fund money box, you should see warning lights flashing: WARNING! WARNING! WARNING! Commence emergency savings mode immediately! Declare a moratorium on all spending except on critical things like giving, the mortgage, utilities, insurance, and groceries (but no eating out). If necessary, have a massive garage sale, work a second job—you name it, just do it. Work on this as quickly as possible, but keep up with your regular payments on current debt obligations and other expenses.

Also, until you have an emergency fund established, don't fund your 401(k), 403(b), or IRA. Don't put away money for your children to go to college, go on vacation, buy new clothes, eat out, expand your cell phone plan, try to wipe out your credit card debt, prepay your mortgage, or buy a new car. *Oh really?* That's right! Be aggressive in building your emergency fund. It may only take a couple of months, and it is vitally important.

Key Point: Without an emergency fund, you will either borrow money from another money box on your MAP or you'll resort to using debt that you cannot pay off at the end of the month when you encounter a major car repair or medical bill. Don't put yourself in that spot. Plan ahead and have emergency funds available.

Priority 3: Eliminate Credit Card Debt and Other Consumer Debt

Once you are faithfully giving at least 10 percent and have your emergency fund established, your next priority will be to eliminate consumer debt—*permanently*. Once again, you will not be putting any money into savings at this time but will be allocating *all of your available funds* toward wiping out your consumer debt, such as all your credit card balances, medical bills, and personal or family loans. The only time you will "save" during this phase of the plan will be to replenish any funds you are forced to spend out of your emergency fund.

Pay off smaller credit card balances first, no matter what the interest rate. In other words, if you have five credit cards with balances of $100; $250; $1,500; $2,000; and $4,000, eliminate the smallest amounts first. Once you pay off your first credit card, begin sending the money you were paying on the first card to help pay off the second card. Once the second card is paid off, allocate all the money to pay off the third card. Continue this process until all the cards are paid in full. Depending on the amount of your debt, this may not be accomplished quickly, unless you are really committed to finding money to pay off these debts. However, by paying off the smaller balances first, you'll gain some momentum for tackling the larger ones.

Key Point: The reason you want to pay off consumer debt at this point is because these accounts usually carry a higher interest rate than your car loans or home mortgage. Also, in most cases the amount owed in consumer or credit card debt is less than the amount owed on car loans or mortgages and is therefore easier to eliminate.

Priority 4: Pay Off Your Car Debt

Now that you have established your top three priorities, your next step is to pay off the cars. To do this, take the money you were allocating to pay off your consumer debts (see Priority 3) and use these funds to eliminate your car debt. At this point, you are still not prepaying your mortgage, investing in stocks or mutual funds, or funding your 401(k), 403(b), or IRA.

Once your car has been paid off, establish a "Cars for Cash" money box on your MAP and start the very next month to *save* the same amount you had been paying to the bank for your car payment. If you keep driving your present car for another three years and keep paying yourself a car payment each month, when the time comes to purchase your next car, *you'll be able to pay cash*—which means no more interest payments! If you continue with this "cars for cash" plan over a span of years, eventually you might actually get a car for free. How? By eliminating the interest expense from your car purchases and earning interest on your savings. It is amazing what a difference it makes to be *earning* interest rather than paying it!

Here's an example of how it works: On a $20,000 car, you can save approximately 25 percent ($5,000) by eliminating interest payments and earning interest on your car savings account. If you saved and earned $5,000 in interest on each car, your total savings in real dollars out of your checking account after buying four cars would be $20,000, which would be enough to purchase another car.

Key Point: The reason for paying off car loans *after* you've paid off your credit cards is that credit cards typically have higher interest rates, and it makes sense to retire the higher-cost debts first. Also, most credit card expenditures are for items we no longer have or that have little or no residual value. For example, after you've worn a set of clothes, how much could you sell them for? Practically nothing. However, when you buy a car, even though it depreciates in value, it does retain some value over the years. It makes sense to pay off credit card debt and car loans before beginning an investment plan because it is to your long-term financial advantage to eliminate paying interest to the bank.

Priority 5: Expand Your Emergency Reserve Fund

The next step after accomplishing the first four priorities is to expand your emergency fund to equal one month's take-home salary. This expanded emergency fund will give you more financial resources to handle any major financial expense that might come your way—and you won't be tempted to go back to living on credit.

Key Point: I recommend waiting until this point to establish a larger emergency fund because one month's take-home pay represents a significant amount of money, and it will take some time to accomplish this goal. A minimum emergency fund of 3 percent of your annual take-home salary (Priority 2) was relatively easy to accomplish and would cover most unexpected expenses. Now that you have eliminated your credit card and car debt, you will have more funds available to expand your emergency fund. Also, it is prudent to expand this fund before you begin a long-term investment plan.

Priority 6: Begin Your Long-Term Savings/Investment Plan

It makes good biblical and financial sense to establish your giving, establish your minimum emergency fund, pay off your credit cards, pay off your car, and expand your emergency fund before you invest in long-term savings. As I have said for many years, you have to earn the right to invest. Don't begin your investment plan until other aspects of your financial house are in order. However, once your top five priorities are in place, it's time to start working on an investment plan. "The wise man saves for the future, but the foolish man spends whatever he gets" (Proverbs 21:20, TLB).

What is your initial goal? Aim for a minimum of 10 percent of your take-home pay. This amount can be increased later, but start with a goal of 10 percent. You could begin by investing money into your company's pension plan, 401(k), or 403(b); or simply invest in a good mutual fund. Don't put all your eggs in one basket, and make sure that a portion of your money goes into a personal investing plan. In other words, don't put every dollar into a 401(k) or 403(b) pension fund. Pension money will not be available for years; however, money you invest in a good mutual fund for personal use (college education for kids, family needs, etc.) can be obtained whenever you need it. If you are looking for a simple guideline, I recommend an initial investment of 5 percent into your pension plan and 5 percent into your personal savings/investing plan. If you can allocate more than 5 percent into each area—great! Don't limit yourself to a 10 percent goal. No matter how much you save or what the rate of return is on your investments, you will be better off than if you do nothing for the next five or fifty years. However, we have a seventh priority in our simple financial plan (paying off your mortgage), and you'll want to have some money available to allocate for that purpose as well.

Key Point: "Steady plodding brings prosperity; hasty speculation brings poverty" (Proverbs 21:5, TLB).

Priority 7: Pay Off Your Mortgage—Become 100 Percent Debt Free

Once you have solidly established your first six priorities, begin looking for creative ways to prepay your mortgage and own your home debt free. Becoming 100 percent debt free is your goal.

Check with your lender to find out exactly how to prepay your mortgage. The most common way is to add a specific amount to your payment each month. Even adding $25 per month on a $75,000 mortgage can eliminate five years of mortgage payments.

Key Point: If your family is like most, your home mortgage is your single biggest debt. Eliminating the smaller debts first will put you in a better position to pay off your mortgage quickly. Because time is a critical component of any investment strategy, and because it might take ten to twenty years to fully pay off your mortgage, I recommend establishing your minimum (10 percent) long-term savings plan before you begin to pay off your mortgage.

Keeping It Simple

If you will follow this simple financial plan, it should help you establish some priorities as you create your MAP. It doesn't cover everything, but it will get you on the road to putting into practice biblical financial principles. How quickly you travel that road will depend on your commitment to the plan and the resources you have available to pursue these priorities.

As you go through this process, you may discover other priorities that I have not mentioned here. But I've given you the basics and a "big picture" perspective. As I mentioned earlier, this chapter was not intended to offer a comprehensive financial plan. However, it should give you some very simple tracks to run on and some important biblical foundational priorities. It's up to you to work into your MAP such items as food, clothing, basic insurance needs, housing expenses, vacations, and paying for college.

Next we will be addressing the important topic of value-based money management.

CHAPTER SEVEN

Understanding Your Value System
It's Not What You Say, It's What You Do

VALUE-BASED MONEY MANAGEMENT: MORE THAN ANYTHING ELSE, YOUR values will determine how you use the resources that God has entrusted to you. Let me give you some examples.

A common question I receive at my seminars and on call-in radio programs deals with being in debt and giving. The caller will say something like this: "I really don't have the money to tithe right now, but I *really, really* want to. The problem is that I am too deep in debt. What should I do?"

This statement reflects the caller's value system more than he or she realizes. If time allows on these shows, I will usually respond by asking the following questions. The usual response is in italics.

Do you have cable TV in your home? *Yes.*

Do you have an Internet service provider? *Yes.*

Do you eat out more than two times a month?
Well, yes.

Have you been to the movies at least once in the last four weeks? *Yes.*

Do you have a cell phone? *Yes.*

Do any of your kids have a cell phone? *Well, yes.*

How many cell phones does your family have?
Um, four.

Do you subscribe to any magazines or newspapers? *Yes.*

How many? *Three.*

Are you saving any money in a pension plan? *Yes, in my company 401(k) plan.*

What is the market value of the house you are living in? The answer varies, but it is usually well over $125,000.

After the caller has answered yes to all or most of the questions, I explain that we *really can* live without cable TV, Internet service, restaurant meals, movies, cell phones, magazines, and the newspaper. Also, most people could choose to live in a less expensive home and drive a less expensive car if they valued something else more. Typically, the caller is very silent right about now. The truth is, most of the people who ask me "the giving question" are simply not willing to support God's kingdom because they value something else more.

Taking an Honest Look at Your Values

You may have never thought of it this way before, but some families place a higher value on spending $100 per month ($1,200 per year) on cable TV, cell phones, and the Internet than they do on using that same money to support God's kingdom. If people spend money according to their true priorities, it's safe to say that giving is simply not a priority—it has a low value to them.

Look at it in terms of a ratio. The higher value is the item on top of the ratio. Which is the higher value in your life?

$$\frac{\text{Giving}}{\text{Cable TV}} \quad \text{or} \quad \frac{\text{Cable TV}}{\text{Giving}}$$

Please don't misunderstand. I'm not opposed to anyone having cable TV, eating out, having cell phones, reading newspapers, going to movies, or investing for the future. But what I am opposed to is doing all these things and then saying, "I don't have any money to support God's kingdom." In my opinion, that's when people reveal their true value system.

Please don't say, "I don't have the money to support God's work." Instead, be honest and say, "I'm not willing to change my value system in order to support God's work." Or be even more specific and say, "I'm not willing to move to a less expensive house, I'm not willing to drive older cars, I'm not willing to eat out less often, and I'm not willing to change my lifestyle in order to give 10 percent or more of my income back to God." It would be so refreshing if just once someone would make that statement on a radio program. I would still be concerned about their value system, but I would applaud their honesty.

If you're giving less than 10 percent of your income to the work of God's kingdom, what's standing in your way? What are you placing a higher value on? Go ahead and fill in the blank: "I'm not willing to _____ in order to give at least 10 percent of my income back to God." It's kind of sobering, isn't it?

This analysis applies in other areas as well. Which do you value more? Living in a larger house or getting out of credit card debt? Going out to eat several times a week or remodeling your home? Driving an expensive car or buying more clothes? The important thing to understand is this: The decisions you make are determined by your true core values.

Our values are reflected in other areas besides giving. When Janet and I lived in Dallas, we remodeled all the different homes we lived in. We painted rooms and put in new carpet, updated the wallpaper and did some minor carpentry work. At that stage in our lives, remodeling our home was a higher value than dining out frequently or driving a brand-new car. We had friends who made the decision to live in an apartment and eat out more often, have more clothes, and drive new cars. Their decisions reflected their value system, just as our decisions reflected ours. In this case, no one was wrong; we just had differing value systems. For Janet and me, remodeling our home, building up equity, and pursuing a goal of becoming debt free was a higher value than eating out and doing other things. For some of our friends, eating out often and having a busy social life were more important than buying and remodeling a home.

Are you beginning to see how our values are reflected in our spending decisions? When the time comes to create your MAP, these are the kinds of decisions you'll be making. Which is more important, dining out or driving a new car? Driving a new car or buying a house? Subscribing to the daily newspaper or paying for Internet service and getting your news online? Chances are, you'll allocate your resources to a lot of different money boxes, and how you decide to divvy up your income will ultimately reflect your value system.

Most Values Are Not "All or None"
In most cases, our values are not a matter of all or none. For example, during the years when remodeling our home was a high value, we would occasionally dine out at one of our favorite restaurants, Spring Creek Bar-B-Q. *Mmm-mmm,* I can almost smell the ribs and taste the delicious homemade rolls. We did not go every night, nor did we drive up in a brand-new car each time. But every time we did go out, we came home to a house we loved.

Suggested Core Values
I have no intention of telling you what your values should be; however, I would like to suggest two that are based upon Scripture: give generously and stay out of debt.

Giving The more I read and study Scripture, the more convinced I become that an individual or couple must be involved in supporting God's work with their resources. I believe that tithing (giving 10 percent of your income) is a great core value. (See Malachi 3:8-10 for God's challenge in this regard.) I encourage you to give this value a high priority as you create your personal MAP. I am convinced that you cannot live fully in God's economy without faithfully supporting his kingdom.

Staying out of debt Let me make it clear from the outset: I do not believe that debt always equals sin. Yes, there are times when debt can become sin, but not in all cases. However, I know for a fact that debt can lead to bondage. "The rich rules over the poor, and the borrower becomes the lender's slave" (Proverbs 22:7, NASB). I have talked with too many couples who have fallen into the debt trap. I personally believe that one of your core values should be to become 100 percent debt free. However, this will not happen unless you establish it as a value, make it a goal, and work toward it as you create your MAP.

I could suggest other core financial values, but let me leave you with these two: If you faithfully support God's kingdom with your resources and pursue a goal of becoming 100 percent debt free, you will be traveling down the best financial road.

Five Major Value Issues

Although I won't presume to tell you what your values should be in these areas, over the years I have found that most families will have to address five major value issues that deal with finances:

1. Housing (size and cost)

2. Mom (At home or working outside the home?)

3. Giving

4. Children (Christian education or public? Car or no car? Pay for college or not?)

5. Lifestyle (cars, travel, clothes, hobbies)

There are other issues, of course, but not directly related to finances. The decisions you make on these "big five" categories will directly affect the amount of resources you have available for the other "smaller" areas. These five issues are also ones that commonly cause problems in a marriage when the husband and wife disagree.

Key Point: Most money problems in marriage arise out of differing values—not the amount of money a family earns. It's really not the amount of money you are earning that creates problems in a marriage. I have seen couples who make very little income, but because they have the same biblical values, they have a happy and fulfilling marriage. I have known couples who are extremely wealthy and have a happy and fulfilling marriage. I have known couples who earn a limited income but always fight and have a miserable marriage. I have counseled couples making gargantuan sums of money who can never agree on anything. Happy and fulfilled or distressed and miserable? What makes the difference in a marriage? It's not the amount of money but the values of the husband and wife. Naturally, couples who share biblical values are more likely to experience true joy and contentment in life than couples who share worldly values.

Discovering Your Core Values

Now would be a great time to examine your values and change them, if necessary. Here's a simple but very revealing exercise: Pull out your checkbook and look through the register. If you use credit cards a lot, you should also review several months of credit card statements. What do you see? There is no better test to determine your values than to look through your checkbook and credit card statements. How you're spending your money tells the story. I hope you're encouraged and motivated by what you see. But if you're shocked, keep pressing on, my friend. I realize that a few of the things I've said might have caused you some pain. You may even have been tempted to toss this book aside. But believe me, everything I have said is from a heart of love and compassion for you. My hope is that you will accept my advice and prayerfully address your values.

As you create your personal MAP, your value system will become very obvious. As you plan how to use God's resources, you will be reflecting your values. Line by line you will need to weigh the value of option A over option B. This is where you will determine what is "just talk" in your life and what is a real value. I hope this simple explanation helps you better understand core values and how they are reflected in your money allocation decisions.

Now let's get to work on creating your personal MAP.

CHAPTER EIGHT

The MAP Planning Worksheet
Creating Your MAP

NOW THAT THE FOUNDATIONAL PRINCIPLES ARE IN PLACE, IT'S TIME TO actually begin the process of creating your Money Allocation Plan. Before we put pencil to paper, however, I strongly encourage you to set this book aside and spend some time praying for God's wisdom and direction. If you're married, get together with your spouse to pray. If you will take time to pray and then invest the necessary time to establish your MAP, you'll be well on your way to a successful financial plan.

Here is an overview of the MAP Planning Worksheet process:

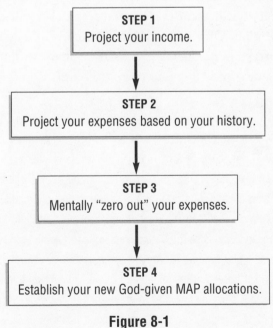

Figure 8-1

One word of advice before you read the rest of the chapter: Do not become overwhelmed with creating the MAP Planning Worksheet. Any new exercise can look complex when you first see it. But once you understand how simple the MAP Planning Worksheet really is, you'll appreciate what a great tool it is. This will be the most time-consuming aspect of developing your MAP, but it will be time well spent. Hang in there with me. You will only have to fill out the MAP Planning Worksheet once.

Furthermore, I am convinced that creating and using a MAP will be easier than you expect and that the resulting spiritual growth will be a blessing in your life and for the kingdom of God. After all, creating your MAP is really more of a spiritual exercise than a financial one. I trust that you're beginning to see it that way.

I recommend that you invest several hours in creating your MAP. I would like to see some spiritual sweat at this point in the process. Could you do this step in a few minutes? Sure. But the quality of your MAP will be a direct reflection of the time you spend developing it. If you shortcut these initial steps, you will short-circuit your overall plan. Once your MAP is developed, it will take only thirty or forty minutes per week to keep it up to date, but you should set aside several hours or more to complete your first MAP.

Key Point: The more time you invest in the initial planning process, the better your MAP will be. Wise planning will greatly increase the potential for your MAP to work. If you invest only thirty or forty minutes at this stage, you will be destined for failure. But if you take the time up front to create a good MAP, it will keep you on the right road, alleviate a lot of stress, and help you to be a good and faithful steward of God's resources. Most budgets fail because not enough time is invested in the planning step or because the budget system is too complex. I recommend that you spend an entire evening (or maybe several evenings) working on the MAP Planning Worksheet. After your initial planning time, you will want to set the MAP aside and come back several days later to prayerfully review your worksheet and make any necessary changes before you create your final MAP.

I remember the first time Janet and I created our MAP. We established our history of income and expenses, projected our income for the next year, made a list of all our planned MAP money boxes, and put a dollar amount next to each one. When we totaled up our planned allocations, they *greatly exceeded* our projected income. This will very likely be true for you as well. In fact, for 99.98 percent of the people who do this exercise, planned expenses will exceed projected income. If your total expenses are *less* than your total income, you are extraordinary! But if you're like most people, you will have to do some cutting for one simple reason: You're not the federal government! Therefore, you must balance the budget— no deficit spending allowed. This MAP Planning Worksheet will help you get your expenditures in line with your income.

Let's begin the process of creating your MAP. On the next four pages, you will find a sample MAP Planning Worksheet already filled out. Carefully study it and then read the instructions on the pages that follow. Don't get bogged down analyzing this example. Instead, spend your time working with your own income and expenses, using the blank MAP Planning Worksheet at the end of the chapter (pages 74–77). Don't be overwhelmed. You'll soon discover just how simple the process really is.

MAP Guidelines

Giving	10% +	Travel/Recreation/Social	2–5%
Savings	5–10%	Clothing	5–7%
Housing	20–40%	Medical	5–10%
Food	10–17%	Personal Allowances	1–5%
Debt Repayment	0–6%	Household Items	2–5%
Transportation	5–15%	Gifts	2–5%
Insurance: Life/		Children	1–10%
Disability/Health	1–4%	Miscellaneous	1–5%

These are simply guidelines. Based on your income, values, priorities, and season of life—single, married, children (and their ages), etc.—you might be under or over these guidelines. Your main goal is to prayerfully consider each category and allocate what you believe is honoring to God, not what a suggested guideline might state.

How to Project Your Monthly Expenses

1. Your goal is to determine how much you need to allocate monthly into each category.

> How to determine the Monthly $ Needed:
> If expenses are annual, divide by 12.
> If expenses are semiannual, divide by 6.
> If expenses are quarterly, divide by 3.
> If expenses are monthly, no need to divide.

2. Total up Monthly $ Needed column for each category.
3. Add all category totals to determine Grand Total on last page.
4. Divide each individual category total by the Grand Total to determine % of Total for each category.
5. Compare your category percents to the MAP guidelines above.
6. Revise if necessary.

To order MAP forms and other resources: www.foundationsforliving.org

Income Projections

	Monthly	Quarterly	Semiannual	Annual	Average $ Monthly
Salary	4,500				4,500
Misc. Earnings	400				400
Total Monthly Income					**$4,900**

Expense Projections

	Monthly	Quarterly	Semiannual	Annual	Monthly $ Needed	% of Total
Giving						
Local Church	490				490	
Ministry	100				100	
Totals					$590	12.0%
Savings						
Emergency Fund	100				100	
Retirement (IRA)				3,000	250	
College						
Totals					$350	7.1%
Housing						
Mortgage/Rent	1,000				1,000	
Home Insurance						
Taxes						
Electricity	100				100	
Gas/Heat	50				50	
Water/Garbage	20				20	
Cable TV	20				20	
Telephone	50				50	
Repairs				1,200	100	
Yard						
Totals					$1,340	27.3%
Food						
Groceries	600				600	
Eat Out	100				100	
Children						
Totals					$700	14.3%

	Monthly	Quarterly	Semiannual	Annual	Monthly $ Needed	% of Total
Debt Repayment						
Credit Card						
Totals					$0	0%
Transportation						
Car Payment						
Car Savings	200				200	
Insurance			360		60	
Gasoline	120				120	
Maintenance & Repairs				540	45	
Totals					$425	8.7%
Insurance						
Life				1,020	85	
Health						
Disability						
Totals					$85	1.7%
Travel/ Recreation/Social						
Social Expenses	100				100	
Club Membership						
Vacations				1,200	100	
Baby-sitting						
Travel						
Sports	50				50	
Totals					$250	5.1%
Clothing						
Single						
Husband				1,200	100	
Wife				1,200	100	
Children				1,200	100	
Totals					$300	6.1%
Medical						
Doctor/Hospital						
Dental						
Eye						
Deductibles				750	63	
Totals					$63	1.3%

	Monthly	Quarterly	Semiannual	Annual	Monthly $ Needed	% of Total
Personal Allowances						
Single						
Husband	100				100	
Wife	100				100	
Children	50				50	
Totals					$250	5.1%
Household Items						
Furniture				1,000	83	
Appliances						
Decorations						
Totals					$83	1.7%
Gifts						
Birthday				400	33	
Wedding/Shower				60	5	
Anniversary				240	20	
Christmas				500	42	
Totals					$100	2.0%
Children						
School Expenses				400	33	
Activities	75				75	
Camps/Trips				220	18	
Sports	50				50	
Lessons	50				50	
Totals					$226	4.6%
Miscellaneous						
Miscellaneous					138	
Totals					$138	2.8%
Grand Total					**$4,900**	**100%**

Step 1: Project your income.

The first step is to determine how much income you expect to receive each month in the coming year. Evaluate past income records, paychecks, and deposits to determine this amount. You will record this information in the Income Projections area of the planning worksheet (see page 75). Fill out this section first.

Step 2: Project your expenses based on your history.

Your goal for this second step is to determine how you have been spending your resources. What is your history? How much have you been spending for food, housing, transportation, and clothes, etc? Go through your checkbook register and credit card statements and calculate your expenditures in the various categories that make up your past expenses. Without a valid history, it will be almost impossible for you to develop a good plan for the future. Once you know where you've been, it will be easier to plan where you want to go. Remember, you will only have to do this step once! After your initial MAP is completed, you'll be looking forward, not back.

Next, you will need to determine how much your expenses have been each month. As the first page of the MAP Planning Worksheet illustrates (see page 74), you will need to divide annual expenses by twelve, semiannual expenses by six, and quarterly expenses by three. For example, if your home property taxes are $1,200 per year, your monthly allocation would be $100 per month ($1,200 ÷ 12 = $100).

Spend sufficient time working on the Expense Projections pages of the MAP Planning Worksheet (see pages 75–77). You might need to go back in the checkbook for six months to obtain some realistic figures. The amounts you write down are only as good as the source they come from. Be sure you do your research; don't just guess at the numbers. This worksheet may take considerable time and effort on your part, but it will be well worth the effort once you have finished.

The Moment of Truth

Once you have determined your projected income and calculated your expenses, see which number is bigger. Do your expenses exceed your income or does your income exceed your projected expenses? As I mentioned before, if you are like most families, your projected expenses will exceed your projected income. If this is true, you will now need to spend time deciding which expenses you can cut back in order for your MAP to balance.

If you are having trouble decreasing your expenses to equal your income, you might want to find out if your projected expenses are within some common guidelines. Notice on the sample MAP Planning Worksheet (see pages 67–69) how each MAP category is totaled and then a percent of the Grand Total is calculated. Look at the Housing category on page 67. The total projected expense for housing is $1,340 and the percent of the total is 27.3 percent ($1,340 housing expense ÷ $4,900 total income = 27.3 percent of total income). Once you have determined your own percentages, you can check them against the guidelines on the first page of the sample MAP Planning Worksheet (see page 66).

Step 3: Zero out your expenses after you finish filling out the worksheet.

After you have carefully completed the MAP Planning Worksheet, it's time to prayerfully evaluate each expense allocation and mentally "zero out" all expense categories. Here is the concept I want you to understand:

> **Nothing** should remain on the MAP worksheet until you have prayerfully justified each planned allocation.

In other words, you have established how you *have been* spending your money, but that doesn't mean you're going to continue to spend your money that way. At this stage, you must zero out each category and then pray about how much—if any—money you will allocate to those categories in the future. Work your way through each MAP allocation category and each item within each category. You will begin with the first allocation on the list: Giving. Next, you will prayerfully evaluate Housing. For the Housing category, you will need to evaluate your expenses for your mortgage, insurance, taxes, electricity, gas, water, cable TV, telephone, repairs, maintenance, and yard work.

There are no sacred cows at this stage of the process. Every expense is subject to prayerful review. Just because you have lived in the same house for ten years does not automatically mean that God wants you to continue living there. Have you recently prayed and asked God if this is where he wants you to continue to live? His answer could be yes, or maybe it will be no. Maybe you really can't afford the house you are living in, and even though it would be emotionally hard to move, it might be the best thing for your family to do. Or maybe you really need more room and you have been postponing the decision. I don't know what you need. But this I do know: It is important for you to evaluate it and pray about it before you make it a part of your new Money Allocation Plan. I want you to have an assurance that you are allocating the resources God has entrusted to you in the best possible way.

Step 4: Establish your new God-given MAP allocations.

Once you have zeroed out your MAP, your next step is to justify every allocation before it becomes a part of your new MAP. Remember, God is not only concerned with what you give; he's concerned with how you spend the entire 100 percent. Here is your opportunity to invite God to be a part of your entire financial life. Again, just because you have always spent your money a certain way does not automatically mean that you will continue to allocate your resources that way on your MAP. What you are looking for are God-approved allocations. With every expense category, pray about it and put it before the Lord before you add it to your MAP.

Take the MAP Planning Worksheet and work your way through each MAP allocation category and each item, line by line. Ask the following questions:

1. Is this a necessity or a desire?

2. What is my real justification for allocating money to this category?

3. Can this expense be totally eliminated?

4. Can this expense be decreased in any way?

5. Do we need to increase the allocation for this area?

By the end of this exercise, you will have decided to increase, decrease, or maintain the same MAP allocations, and you may have eliminated some categories altogether. If you justify every expense before it goes back onto your MAP, you will develop a confidence about where each dollar is going and why. You should have a valid reason for allocating every dollar. Now, using the margins of your MAP Planning Worksheet, pencil in your newly approved allocation amounts.

In the next chapter, you will find a brief commentary for each MAP allocation category and a list of questions to help you further analyze your allocations decisions. Some of the commentary might be helpful as you pray about increasing, decreasing, or eliminating allocations.

MAP Guidelines

Giving	10% +	Travel/Recreation/Social	2–5%
Savings	5–10%	Clothing	5–7%
Housing	20–40%	Medical	5–10%
Food	10–17%	Personal Allowances	1–5%
Debt Repayment	0–6%	Household Items	2–5%
Transportation	5–15%	Gifts	2–5%
Insurance: Life/		Children	1–10%
Disability/Health	1–4%	Miscellaneous	1–5%

These are simply guidelines. Based on your income, values, priorities, and season of life—single, married, children (and their ages), etc.—you might be under or over these guidelines. Your main goal is to prayerfully consider each category and allocate what you believe is honoring to God, not what a suggested guideline might state.

How to Project Your Monthly Expenses

1. Your goal is to determine how much you need to allocate monthly into each category.

> How to determine the Monthly $ Needed:
> If expenses are annual, divide by 12.
> If expenses are semiannual, divide by 6.
> If expenses are quarterly, divide by 3.
> If expenses are monthly, no need to divide.

2. Total up Monthly $ Needed column for each category.
3. Add all category totals to determine Grand Total on last page.
4. Divide each individual category total by the Grand Total to determine % of Total for each category.
5. Compare your category percents to the MAP guidelines above.
6. Revise if necessary.

To order MAP forms and other resources: www.foundationsforliving.org

Income Projections

	Monthly	Quarterly	Semiannual	Annual	Average $ Monthly
Salary					
Misc. Earnings					
Total Monthly Income					$

Expense Projections

	Monthly	Quarterly	Semiannual	Annual	Monthly $ Needed	% of Total
Giving						
Local Church						
Totals					$	%
Savings						
Emergency Fund						
Retirement (IRA)						
College						
Totals					$	%
Housing						
Mortgage/Rent						
Home Insurance						
Taxes						
Electricity						
Gas/Heat						
Water/Garbage						
Cable TV						
Telephone						
Repairs						
Yard						
Totals					$	%
Food						
Groceries						
Eat Out						
Children						
Totals					$	%

	Monthly	Quarterly	Semiannual	Annual	Monthly $ Needed	% of Total
Debt Repayment						
Credit Card						
Totals					$	%
Transportation						
Car Payment						
Car Savings						
Insurance						
Gasoline						
Maintenance & Repairs						
Totals					$	%
Insurance						
Life						
Health						
Disability						
Totals					$	%
Travel/ Recreation/Social						
Social Expenses						
Club Membership						
Vacations						
Baby-sitting						
Travel						
Sports						
Totals					$	%
Clothing						
Single						
Husband						
Wife						
Children						
Totals					$	%
Medical						
Doctor/Hospital						
Dental						
Eye						
Deductibles						
Totals					$	%

	Monthly	Quarterly	Semiannual	Annual	Monthly $ Needed	% of Total
Personal						
Allowances						
Single						
Husband					$	
Wife						
Children						
Totals					$	%
Household Items						
Furniture						
Appliances						
Decorations						
Totals					$	%
Gifts						
Birthday						
Wedding/Shower						
Anniversary						
Christmas						
Totals					$	%
Children						
School Expenses						
Activities						
Camps/Trips						
Sports						
Lessons						
Totals					$	%
Miscellaneous						
Miscellaneous						
Totals					$	%
Grand Total					$	%

CHAPTER NINE

Analyzing Your MAP Categories
Asking the Important Questions

ON THE PAGES THAT FOLLOW, YOU WILL FIND WHAT I HOPE ARE SOME insightful comments on each MAP category. If you are having difficulty cutting your expenses, you should find this chapter helpful as you prayerfully examine each MAP category. I have tried to add some biblical perspectives and ask some very practical questions that you can consider as you allocate money on your MAP.

Giving

This is one area where you definitely want to remain faithful. Don't rob God! If you are not generously supporting God's kingdom, it's time to start. I am convinced that if you are faithful in supporting God's kingdom, he will take what is left over and multiply it for your family. Giving is a step of faith. God only calls us to *give out of what we have received*. If you receive zero dollars in income this year, you have no requirement to give. If you operate on a principle of firstfruits giving and there are no fruits (income), you obviously have no firstfruits to give. However, if you receive $50,000 in income this year, you should give proportionally of your firstfruits. God will honor your faithfulness (see Malachi 3:8-10 and 2 Corinthians 8:1-5).

Questions about Giving
• Is giving a biblical conviction in my life?

• Why do I give?

- To whom should I be giving?

- Do I give of my firstfruits or do I tend to give God the leftovers or nothing?

- Is giving my highest financial priority? Why or why not?

- What has been my giving history over the last twelve months? Has it been honoring to God?

- Which expenses might I need to eliminate in order to become a faithful giver?

Savings

Go back and review the Simple Financial Plan in chapter 6. This will help you establish some priorities in your savings. If you have no savings, then you will be forced to use credit cards when you incur a major car repair, house repair, or medical bill. You must have an emergency fund set aside of at least 3 percent of your annual take-home pay but not less than $500. Eventually, you will want to build up this emergency fund to equal one month's take-home salary.

Questions about Savings

- Do I have a minimum of 3 percent of my annual take-home pay or $500 in an emergency fund?

- Do I save on a regular basis?

- Do I save more or give more each year?

- Do I have a plan for my investments?

- Are my investments properly diversified?

Housing

For most families, housing is the largest expense category, consuming anywhere from 20 percent to 50 percent of their take-home pay. If your housing expense is more than 40 percent of your take-home income, you may need to prayerfully consider moving your family to a less expensive home. I realize that this would be a very hard thing for most families to do, but in reality this action just might be the best thing you've ever done. If you are buying your first home or a new home, be sure to use only one income to qualify for the mortgage.

I do not know God's will for your life, but I do know that you should seriously consider how much of your income you are committing to the Housing category.

Questions about Housing

• Can we really afford the home we are living in?

• Does the mortgage payment consume too much of our income?

• How much of my pride is tied up in our home?

• Am I willing to move if it would help us financially?

• Have I recently asked God if this is the best house for our family?

Mortgage

It might be possible for you to remain in your present home by simply refinancing your mortgage. If interest rates are at least 2 percent lower than your present home mortgage rate, you should check into refinancing. However, be sure you plan to live in your home long enough to cover your refinancing costs. If you refinance, whatever you do, don't enter back into a new thirty-year mortgage!

When you refinance, try to cut years off your mortgage, not add years back onto it.

Questions about Your Mortgage

• Have mortgage interest rates dropped at least 2 percent since we bought our house? If yes, check into refinancing.

• If we refinance, do we have funds to put into our home so we can obtain a smaller mortgage—and therefore have a smaller monthly payment?

Homeowner's Insurance

Talk with your agent about increasing your homeowner's insurance deductible to help lower your premium.

Questions about Homeowner's Insurance

• How much can we save each year by increasing our deductible?

• Have we asked our agent if there are other ways to save on our premium, such as installing smoke alarms or a security system?

Utilities

You might need to do a better job of controlling the thermostat during the day.

Questions about Utilities

• Can we agree to set the heat/air-conditioning on a specific temperature and leave it alone?

• How can we best remember to turn off the heat/cooling when we leave the house?

• Do we have leaking water faucets that need to be repaired?

• Will my utility company average my monthly bill so my payment amount will be more consistent?

Cable TV

Something Janet and I have done on occasion is eliminate the cable TV bill. To be honest, it was great. I can assure you we spent more time together as a family because we did not have cable TV. Some cities offer limited basic cable. It is not *basic*, but *limited basic*. Generally you will never see it advertised, but some states require cable companies to offer it. In our city it costs just under $7.00 per month. Typically, limited basic cable includes the four major networks, one religious channel, one weather channel, and CNN Headline News, but it does not include things like ESPN. It really is limited basic!

Questions about Cable TV

• Does our city offer limited basic cable?

• Do we really need cable TV?

• How much time do we waste watching TV?

• What would life be like if we did not have cable TV? Would we enjoy our family more?

• Would we have more time together as a family?

• Am I willing to give it a try? Why or why not?

• Are my children hooked on watching TV?

Telephone Service

Check to be sure you are with a company that offers the best long-distance rates. Rates are becoming more competitive every day. Also, you might need to work at limiting your long-distance calls to help you save money. E-mail has become a great option for communication. If you have free access to the Internet, it will cost you nothing to send and receive e-mail. If you really need to save money, be sure to eliminate all the extra features on your phone bill, such as call waiting, call forwarding, and caller ID. Just sign up for the basic plan.

Cell phones have become a major expense for many families. I recently talked to one friend who is spending $60 to $100 per month for his cell phone. Maybe using a cell phone has become a way of life for you, but the elimination of a cell phone might have to be one of your sacrifices. Don't just assume you need a cell phone because "everyone carries one these days." If you would like to have a cell phone for emergencies, which is a great thing, consider obtaining an inexpensive basic plan with limited minutes.

Questions about Telephone Service

• Do we really need to have all the features like call waiting, call forwarding, call conferencing, caller ID, three-way calling, and voice mail? Can we get by with just basic phone service?

• Do we really need local phone service? Why? The answer to this one may seem obvious, but ask the question anyway. Are there other options available? For example, could you save money overall by combining your cellular service with your local phone service? In the wake of deregulation, it seems that more and more options for phone service are becoming available.

• Do I really need a cell phone? Why? Does everyone in our family really need to have his/her own cell phone?

• Have we searched for the best long-distance calling plan for our family?

• Have we established guidelines for limiting the cost of long-distance phone calls?

Home Repairs

Maybe being a handyman is not your dream, but in order to cut expenses you might need to learn a few basic skills in plumbing, carpentry, and painting. It will always cost you less to do your own repairs. You should also consider attending free "how to" seminars at your local building-supply store. You can learn how to wallpaper, how to install lighting fixtures, fans, shower enclosures, ceramic tile floors, and how to build a wood deck—just to name a few.

Questions about Home Repairs

• Are there things that we have been paying someone else to do that we can begin doing ourselves?

• Do we have any home improvement projects that we can do on our own?

• If we need specific tools, do we know someone we can borrow them from rather than having to buy them?

• Do we really need to do the home repairs we presently have planned, or can they wait?

• What repairs are critical to do immediately and what is the least expensive way to do them?

• Do we have friends who are handymen we might barter some time with? (For example, you might do their taxes or watch their kids next weekend in exchange for some carpentry work.)

Yard Work

Doing your own yard work can be a real money saver. Just think about it. If you are spending $100 per month for yard care, that equals $1,200 per year.

Questions about Yard Work
• Am I physically able to cut the grass?

• Should the children be working in the yard instead of watching TV or playing on the computer all day?

Food
Becoming a smart shopper can have a radical impact on your food budget. Plan your meals, and make smart shopping trips to the store. Many people don't like coupons, but they can save a bundle over a year's time. For example, if you save $10 per week, that adds up to more than $500 per year.

Questions about Food
• Are we wasting money on food that isn't even good for us?

• How can we best save on our food budget?

Eating Out
This is one area where most families can cut back. Eating out just two to four times a month could cost more than $100 per month, or $1,200 per year. Let me encourage you to carefully track how much you spend eating out during the next four weeks and use that information to make a wise plan for the future.

Questions about Eating Out
• Can we really afford to eat out?

• Do we really need to eat out as often as we do? Why?

• How much is the maximum we should spend each month on eating out?

• If we are going to eat out, could we save money by eating at less expensive restaurants?

Children's Food

School lunches and frequent trips to fast-food restaurants can be very expensive.

Questions about Children's Food

• How much are we spending on fast food and other meals away from home for our kids?

• Have we set a limit for how much our children can spend on fast food each week or month?

• Is it less expensive for our children to take their lunch to school or buy it from the school?

Debt Repayment

This category is used for credit card bills that are not paid in full, school loans, medical bills, and other consumer debt. The more money you allocate to this category, the faster you will become debt free.

Questions about Debt Repayment

• What is the maximum amount we can allocate to this category?

• How soon can we have all these debts paid off?

• Have we stopped overspending, or is it still a problem?

Transportation

Be creative in looking for ways to cut your expenses. Consider buying used cars instead of new cars. Talk to your car insurance agent about lowering your premium by increasing your deductible. Talk to your neighbors about carpooling to school or work.

Questions about Transportation
• Are we driving a car we really cannot afford?

• Have we seriously considered selling it and reducing our cost?

• Can we really afford for our teenagers to have their own car?

• Do we qualify for a good student or driver's ed discount?

• Have we asked our agent how we can decrease our premium?

Health and Life Insurance

Do not risk going for one day without health insurance! With the cost of medical care, this is one area you cannot eliminate. Make sure you have adequate life insurance, but be careful not to be overinsured. Always carefully compare rates for all your insurance needs. Don't just pay the premium when it arrives; go ahead and call three other companies for comparable quotes.

Questions about Health and Life Insurance
• Have we called three different insurance companies for quotes?

• Have we asked our agent how we can decrease our premium?

• Do we have too much life insurance? Are we overinsured?

• Do we need more life insurance? Are we underinsured?

Travel, Recreation, and Social Expenses

Be creative in this area. This can become a black hole for your money. Do you hear that sucking sound of all the money going into this money pit? I am not going to beat you up on all the different areas—you already know what they are.

Questions about Travel, Recreation, and Social Expenses
• Can we afford to be members of clubs?

• How much can we really afford to spend on vacations?

• How can we save on baby-sitting expenses?

• Are we spending too much on social events when we have other important needs?

Clothing

Be sure you are operating on a specific clothing budget, and don't overspend it. Try to find great sales and good values. Most of us on a limited budget cannot afford to buy $125 tennis shoes but must settle for the $50 no-name brand. By the way, they wear just as great. Buying generic or store brands might be one of the ways your family will need to sacrifice. Shopping at outlet malls, even for brand names, is a great way to save money.

Questions about Clothing
• How much can I really afford to spend on clothing?

• Can I shop at outlet malls?

• Do I have a budget before I go shopping?

Medical Expenses

If you are paying for your own health insurance, one way to decrease your monthly expenses is to have your deductible increased. For example, a monthly health insurance premium with a $250 annual deductible for a family of four might cost $600 per month. By increasing the deductible to $1000, the monthly cost might drop the premium to $400 per month—a savings of $200 per month. Do you think you will be spending more than $200 per month in doctor visits and prescriptions? If not, this might be a good way to lower your expenses.

Questions about Medical Expenses
• Can we raise our health insurance deductible and save money?

• Can we buy our eyeglasses when they are on sale?

Personal Allowances
Everyone needs to have a personal allowance, even if it is small. Your personal allowance money is used for things personal to you and not necessarily for the entire family.

Questions about Personal Allowances
• Realistically, how much does each person need for his or her personal allowance?

• Have I prayed about how much I am spending in this area?

House—General (Furniture, Appliances, and Decorations)
My advice—never use long-term debt to purchase furniture or decorations. Save up and pay cash!

Questions about Furniture, Appliances, and Decorations
• Are we living within our financial means when we purchase furniture or appliances?

• Do I need to pray more about being content?

Gifts
My suggestion is that you make a list of all the gifts you need to purchase during the year for immediate and extended family. Be sure to include birthdays, Christmas, and anniversaries. Prayerfully write an amount next to each gift and calculate the grand

total. Establish an amount to spend and do not exceed it. In large families or extended families you might consider drawing names instead of buying every person a present.

Questions about Gifts
• How much am I spending on gifts?

• Can I really afford to be spending this much on gifts?

Children

If you have children, you already know that this area of your MAP is very important. My advice is to live within your means. If you overspend on your kids and accumulate a lot of debt, everyone—including the children—will suffer in the coming years. Learn to pace yourself financially. Buy the things your children need, not everything they want. Give them guidelines for how much you will spend on activities, camps, sports, and so on.

Questions about Spending on Your Children
• How many activities should we allow our children to be involved in?

• Am I making my decisions based on what we can afford or what other families are doing?

• If my teenagers need more spending money, have I helped them to find a job?

• Do I model financial responsibility to my children?

Miscellaneous

This is the category you will need to carefully plan and monitor. Be sure you adequately fund this category or you will find it to be a real budget-buster.

Conclusion

There is no magical or simple formula to make this procedure easy. Projecting your monthly living expenses is a time-consuming task but well worth the effort. Your goal is to create a MAP that you can live on and that brings honor to God.

CHAPTER TEN

Month-by-Month Mapping
The Basics of Using Your MAP

IN THIS CHAPTER, YOU WILL LEARN HOW TO ACTUALLY USE YOUR MAP EACH month. Most MAP users take about thirty to forty minutes each week to completely update their MAP and remain totally on top of their financial lives.

Just think about it. Only thirty minutes per week to accomplish what most people are looking for—financial control. With the MAP system, you are on the road to

- having less stress

- having fewer fights

- paying all your bills on time

- never worrying about bouncing checks

- increasing your ability to give

- increasing your capacity to save

- finding true freedom in your spending

It may be hard to believe how one piece of paper each month can be so helpful—but it works! The number one response I hear from MAP users is, "This is so simple!" You don't need to be an accountant or have an MBA to keep up with your personal finances.

The MAP form is your key to success. This simple worksheet is the key to making the MAP system work on a daily basis. This could be the simple budgeting system you have been looking for all these years. Even if you have tried other plans and failed, I think you will find the MAP system is different.

By now you should have filled out your MAP Planning Worksheet, zeroed out your expense allocations, established your new MAP allocation categories, and designated the amount of money you plan to allocate into each MAP money box every month. Now you are ready to learn how to use the MAP each month.

On the next four pages, you will find a sample MAP. Refer to this sample frequently as you read the information in this chapter. Remember that the real MAP forms are on a single sheet of paper, 11″ × 17″, folded once to make up four 8½″ × 11″ pages. All you will need is twelve forms per year (one per month) to use the MAP system. At the end of the chapter, you will find information on how to order your Start-up MAP Kit, which includes a one-year supply of full-size MAP forms.

Let me encourage you to take plenty of time as you work your way through this chapter. Try to read it in one session. Focus on understanding the big picture. If you are confused by anything— don't keep reading; instead, go back and reread the instructions. Master the simple MAP form and master your financial life! You can do it!

Month: March   **Year:** 2003

MAP Money Box	MAP Planned Amount	Actual Deposits into Checking Account during Month and Allocated into MAP Money Boxes According to Plan					
Allocation	$4,900 Total for Month	$2,450 3/1	$2,450 3/15	$	$	$	$
Giving	590	295	295				
Emergency Fund	100	100					
Retirement (IRA)	250		250				
Mortgage	1,000	1,000					
Electricity	100		100				
Gas/Heat	50		50				
Water	20		20				
Cable TV	20		20				
Telephone	50		50				
Home Repairs	100		100				
Food	600	600					
Eat Out	100	50	50				
Car Savings	200		200				
Car Insurance	60		60				
Car Gasoline	120	120					
Car Maintenance & Repairs	45		45				
Life Insurance	85		85				
Social	100		100				
Vacations	100		100				
Sports	50		50				
Husband Clothes	100		100				
Wife Clothes	100		100				
Children Clothes	100		100				
Medical	63		63				
Husband Allowance	100	100					
Wife Allowance	100	100					
Children Allowance	50		50				
Household Items	83		83				
Gifts	100		100				
Children	226	85	141				
Miscellaneous	138		138				

To order MAP forms and other resources: www.foundationsforliving.org

Mortgage			
D/#	+	–	=
BB			0
3/1	1,000		1,000
512		1,000	0

Electricity			
D/#	+	–	=
BB			37
3/15	100		137
516		125	12

Gas/Heat			
D/#	+	–	=
BB			11
3/15	50		61
517		41	20

Water			
D/#	+	–	=
BB			7
3/15	20		27
518		21	6

Life Insurance			
D/#	+	–	=
BB			170
3/15	85		255

Husband Clothes			
D/#	+	–	=
BB			205
509		75	130
3/15	100		230
533		15	215

Wife Clothes			
D/#	+	–	=
BB			315
CC		124	191
3/15	100		291

Children Clothes			
D/#	+	–	=
BB			75
3/15	100		175
534		65	110
547		19	91

Cable TV			
D/#	+	–	=
BB			0
3/15	20		20
519		20	0

Telephone			
D/#	+	–	=
BB			21
3/15	50		71
520		48	23

Vacations			
D/#	+	–	=
BB			200
3/15	100		300

Sports			
D/#	+	–	=
BB			0
3/15	50		50
548		50	0

Social			
D/#	+	–	=
BB			15
3/15	100		115
513		25	90
536		25	65
549		25	40

Husband Allowance			
D/#	+	–	=
BB			60
3/1	100		160
507		50	110
521		50	60
537		50	10
Food	20		30

Wife Allowance			
D/#	+	–	=
BB			45
3/1	100		145
544		50	95
550		50	45

Children Allowance			
D/#	+	–	=
BB			0
3/15	50		50
538		25	25
540		25	0

Food

D/#	+	−	=
BB			21
3/1	600		621
502		111	510
510		79	431
511		37	394
515		105	289
522		78	211
530		134	77
531		12	65
539		20	45
551		19	26
H.A.		20	6

Miscellaneous

D/#	Item	+	−	=
BB				85
503	Stamps		10	75
504			12	63
	Balance MAP	2		65
508			19	46
3/15		138		184
	Balance MAP		1	183
546			10	173
	Balance MAP	3		176
552			21	155
	Balance MAP		2	153

Home Repairs

D/#	Item	+	−	=
BB				225
3/15		100		325
535	Plumber		75	250

Giving

D/#	Item	+	−	=
BB				0
3/1			295	295
501	Church		295	0
3/15			295	295
524	Church		195	100
525			100	0

Eat Out

D/#	+	−	=
BB			0
3/1	50		50
CC		42	8
3/15	50		58

Gifts

D/#	+	−	=
BB			200
3/15	100		300
523		50	250

Emergency Fund

D/#	+	−	=
BB			400
3/1	100		500

Credit Cards

D/#	Item	Transfer From (Name of MAP Money Box)	Name of Card	PD	+	−	=
BB							100
3/2	Gas	Car Gasoline	MC		20		120
3/5	Olive Garden	Eat Out	MC		42		162
3/9	Fashion Tree	Wife Clothes	MC		124		286
529	Payment of CC Bill		MC			100	186

REMEMBER: IT'S IMPOSSIBLE TO TAKE MONEY OUT OF AN EMPTY MONEY BOX!

Car Savings			
D/#	+	–	=
BB			400
3/15	200		600

Car Insurance			
D/#	+	–	=
BB			120
3/15	60		180

Car Maintenance & Repairs				
D/#	Item	+	–	=
BB				516
505	New Tires		296	220
514	Oil Change		24	196
3/15		45		241

Car Gasoline			
D/#	+	–	=
BB			25
3/1	120		145
CC		20	125

Household Items			
D/#	+	–	=
BB			124
506		20	104
3/15	83		187
526		21	166
532		49	117
553		37	80

Company Reimbursement				
D/#	Item	+	–	=
BB				

Retirement (IRA)			
D/#	+	–	=
BB			750
3/15	250		1,000
541		1,000	0

D/#	+	–	=
BB			

Medical				
D/#	Item	+	–	=
BB				126
3/15			63	189
542	Dr. Smith		40	149

Children			
D/#	+	–	=
BB			40
3/1	85		125
527		62	63
3/15	141		204
528		45	159
543		31	128
545		8	120

D/#	+	–	=
BB			

Debt Repayment				
D/#	Item	+	–	=
BB				

The Front Page of the MAP

I will begin by explaining the front page of the MAP. As you read this section, refer to page 95.

Month and Year

At the very top of each MAP form, you will find a place to record the month and year for the current MAP. Just think about it—on only twelve sheets of paper you will be able to completely manage your financial affairs.

MAP Money Box Allocation and MAP Planned Amount

The first two columns on the MAP form are for you to record your allocation categories and the specific dollar amount you plan to allocate into each one every month. Refer back to the sample MAP Planning Worksheet on pages 66–69 to see how we simply transferred the specific MAP items and dollar amounts from the worksheet to the MAP form. The grand total from the MAP Planning Worksheet in our example was $4,900 per month. The MAP Planned Amount on the MAP form in this chapter is also $4,900. The MAP Planned Amount should equal your total monthly take-home pay. In other words, you are saying, "I plan to receive $4,900 in income this month, and I plan to allocate/distribute this money into the following thirty-one MAP money boxes."

Actual Deposits

The third section on the front page of the MAP form is where you will record money that you have deposited into your checking account. Do not record any amounts in this section until you have actually received the money and made the deposit.

Each time you make a deposit, record it in the first available deposit column in the chart. The example on page 95 shows a family receiving $2,450 on March 1, so we have recorded the amount and the date in the first column of the Actual Deposits section. If you receive more than one paycheck each month, you must decide which MAP money boxes you want to disperse funds into from each paycheck. You can fully fund a specific MAP category from one paycheck, or you may fund it partially out of each paycheck. In our example, you can see that the $2,450 deposited on March 1 was allocated into nine MAP money boxes: Giving = $295; Emergency Fund = $100; Mortgage = $1000; Food = $600; Eat Out = $50; Car Gasoline = $120; Husband Allowance = $100; Wife Allowance = $100; and Children = $85. The total of these nine allocations equals $2,450.

If you receive more than one paycheck per month, it will take more time to update your MAP the first few months because the whole process is new and you will have to decide which MAP categories need to be funded from each paycheck. However, you will soon develop a regular routine for how each paycheck will be distributed.

Transferring Funds from the MAP Front Page to the Money Boxes

Once you have decided how you want to allocate your paycheck, you then transfer each amount into the corresponding money boxes on the two inside pages and the back page of your MAP (see pages 96–98). Let's look at how this is done.

On the front page of the sample MAP form (see page 95), look at the third column, which shows our first deposit of $2,450 on 3/1. Notice that our first allocation is $295 for Giving. Now look at the page on the sample MAP form that includes the Giving money box (see page 97). What do you see? The BB (beginning balance) is $0, $295 is recorded in the (+) column, and there is a balance of $295 in the (=) column.

The next allocation from our 3/1 paycheck is for the Emergency Fund. Find the Emergency Fund money box on the sample MAP form (see page 97). What do you see? The BB (beginning balance) is $400, we added $100 in the (+) column, which brings the balance in the (=) column to $500. We now have $500 available for emergencies.

The next allocations are $1,000 into the Mortgage money box,

$600 into the Food money box, $50 into the Eat Out money box, $120 into the Car Gasoline money box, $100 into the Husband Allowance money box, $100 into the Wife Allowance money box, and $85 into the Children money box. You can find the corresponding money boxes on the sample MAP form (see pages 96–98) and see how these allocations were transferred.

Helpful Hint: As you transfer each dollar amount into the MAP money boxes, you might want to place a small check mark next to each amount on the front page, showing that you have transferred this money into the MAP system.

Rounding to Whole Dollar Amounts When using the MAP categories, round your entries to the nearest whole dollar. Notice how this has been done on the sample MAP form. Rounding will save you hours every month. You do not need to keep your MAP to the penny. However, be sure to keep your checkbook register to the penny.

The Inside and Back Pages of the MAP

Before we continue, let me explain a few things about the MAP money boxes (see pages 96–98). The first thing you may notice is that the boxes are all different sizes. This is because different-size categories are to be used for different purposes. The larger ones are for categories that will likely have multiple entries, such as food. I don't know about your family, but we write more checks to the grocery store than anywhere else. The small boxes are for budget categories that usually have only one or two entries each month, such as Mortgage, Insurance, or Long-Term Savings.

D/# Column

Notice how each money box has a variety of columns. The first column is the "D/#" column. This is to be used for either the date or the check number. I recommend that you use dates for deposits (income allocations) and check numbers for expenditures (expense allocations) in each money box.

Beginning Balance (BB)

The BB on the first line of each money box stands for "beginning balance." At the end of each month, you will transfer the ending balance in each money box to the BB line of the corresponding money box for the next month's MAP.

(+) Column

Use the (+) column when you are allocating money into your MAP money boxes. For example, look at the MAP Food money box on the sample MAP form (see page 97). In the D/# column, you see 3/1, representing March 1, and $600 in the (+) column. This tells you that on March 1, we allocated $600 into our MAP Food money box.

(–) Column

Use the (–) column when you spend money out of a MAP money box. Look again at the Food money box. In the D/# column you will see 502. You will also see $111 in the (–) column and $510 in the (=) column. This tells us we wrote check number 502 for $111 and we have $510 remaining dollars to be spent for food this month. If for some reason you wanted to find out which store you wrote the check to and when it was dated, you could go to your checkbook register and look up check number 502.

(=) Column

The first entry in the (=) column shows the beginning balance (BB) for the month. For example, in the Food money box, we had $21 left over when February ended. Therefore, we simply transferred the ending food balance of $21 to the beginning balance for the Food money box for March. The (=) column tells you how much money you have remaining in your money box. If it has a balance, you have money available to spend. If this column has a 0, you do not have any money to spend in this category until you allocate more money into it. Remember, it is impossible to take money out of an empty box.

Item Column

Look at the Home Repairs, Giving, and Miscellaneous money boxes on page 97. Notice how these categories have an additional column titled Item. This space can be used to make a notation of how or where the funds were spent.

Credit Cards

As you might imagine, the Credit Cards category is very important. Look at the Credit Cards money box on the sample MAP form (see page 97), and let's discuss the first transaction.

On March 2, we filled up our car with gasoline and charged the gas on our MasterCard. When we update our MAP at the end of the week, we record this charge and budget the expense in the following way:

Put the date, 3/2, in the D/# column of the Credit Cards money box. This corresponds to the date you actually made the purchase. It is very helpful to have the purchase date when the bill arrives in the mail.

Next, in the Item column, write "Gas" or the store name. This tells you what you purchased or where you shopped.

Next, in the Transfer From column, put the name of the MAP money box from which you are withdrawing the money. In our example, our purchase was for gas, so the money will come out of our Car Gasoline money box. This exercise reinforces the realization that even though this is a credit card purchase, you have still spent money. Consequently, money must be taken out of the Car Gasoline money box and moved into our Credit Cards money box.

Finally, put the name of the card (MC, for MasterCard) in the Name of Card column. This will help you when it comes time to pay all the MasterCard charges.

Now look at the Car Gasoline money box on the sample MAP form (see page 98). You will find the letters CC in the D/# column. This indicates a credit card transfer. Notice the $20 in the (−) column, which indicates that we are taking $20 out of the Car Gasoline money box and transferring it into the Credit Cards money box. We now have $125 remaining in our Car Gasoline money box.

To return to our post office analogy for a moment, we are simply "forwarding" the money from one address to another. The money was originally addressed to the Car Gasoline money box, but now it is being forwarded to a new address: the Credit Cards money box.

Another result of this transfer is that we now have more money in our Credit Cards money box, so that when the bill arrives, we already have enough money in our Credit Cards money box to pay it. We record the charge amount ($20) in the (+) column of the Credit Cards money box. This might seem strange, putting what we charged in the (+) column, but this is exactly what we need to do. Remember, we just took $20 out of the Car Gasoline money box, and now we are putting it into the Credit Cards money box until the bill comes and we need to take it out.

The balance in the Credit Cards money box is now $120. In our example, $100 was the beginning balance brought forward from the previous month. In other words, we already had $100 in our Credit Cards money box from charges last month. This money will be used to pay the credit card bill that will arrive later this month. When the bill comes, we go back to last month's budget and place a check mark in the Paid column (PD) beside each entry that is being paid. Then we write the check to MasterCard.

Look in the D/# column on the Credit Cards money box and find where we recorded check number 529. Note that the $100 recorded in the (–) column corresponds to the credit card charges from the previous month, which would show up on this month's credit card statement. When the credit card bill is paid, the new balance of $186 is recorded in the (=) column. The $186 balance in the Credit Cards money box represents the total of all outstanding credit card charges we have made this month.

It is best if you update your credit card charges weekly to keep all your money boxes up to date. If you do not reflect your credit card charges immediately, it will be easy to overspend because it takes most credit card bills twenty-five to thirty days to arrive in your mailbox. By updating your credit card expenses weekly, you know exactly how much you actually have available to spend in each money box.

MAP Money Boxes Reflect Your Checkbook

Look at it this way:

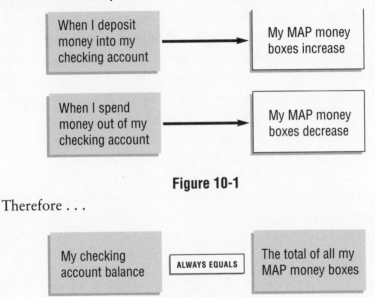

| When I deposit money into my checking account | → | My MAP money boxes increase |

| When I spend money out of my checking account | → | My MAP money boxes decrease |

Figure 10-1

Therefore . . .

| My checking account balance | ALWAYS EQUALS | The total of all my MAP money boxes |

Figure 10-2

Updating the MAP Weekly

Either Janet or I will update our MAP once a week. We sit down with our checkbook, the MAP, a pencil, and a calculator. This is when we record on our MAP all the financial activities that took place in our checkbook during the week.

The updating must take place at least weekly to let us know how we are doing in all our MAP categories. In my opinion, if you only update your MAP once a month, you are simply wasting your time. Instead of budgeting, you are spending a lot of time tracking where all the money went!

Each week when you sit down with your checkbook to update the budget categories, put a check mark next to each entry in your checkbook documenting that the expense item has been recorded in the MAP. Next week, when you update the budget again, you will know precisely where to begin.

Balancing the Budget Weekly

Here's an important guideline for making the MAP work: The total balance of all your MAP categories should *equal* the balance in your checkbook. Look again at our sample MAP form. If we add up all the ending balances for every money box, the total is $4,226, which should equal the amount we have in our checkbook. As deposits are made into our checking account, we allocate the money into the appropriate MAP money boxes. As we spend money out of our checkbook, we take money out of our money boxes.

Key Point: As money goes into your checkbook, your MAP total increases.

As money goes out of your checkbook, your MAP total decreases.

Summary of Ending Balances from Our Sample MAP

Mortgage	$0	Social	$40
Electricity	$12	H. Allowance	$30
Gas/Heat	$20	W. Allowance	$45
Water	$6	C. Allowance	$0
Life Insurance	$255	Food	$6
H. Clothes	$215	Miscellaneous	$153
W. Clothes	$291	Home Repairs	$250
C. Clothes	$91	Giving	$0
Cable TV	$0	Eat Out	$58
Telephone	$23	Gifts	$250
Vacations	$300	Emergency Fund	$500
Sports	$0	Credit Cards	$186

Car Savings $600	Retirement (IRA) $0
Car Insurance $180	Medical $149
Car Maintenance	Children $120
and Repairs $241	**MAP Total $4,226**
Car Gasoline $125	**Checkbook Balance = Total of**
Household Items $80	**All MAP Categories**

Differences Due to Rounding

When we add up the ending balances for all the MAP money boxes, the grand total should equal the balance in our checkbook. However, due to rounding, we might have a difference of a few dollars, plus or minus.

If the MAP total is *less* than your checkbook balance, *add* the difference to your Miscellaneous money box. Refer to the Miscellaneous money box on our sample MAP form (see page 97). Notice the notation in the Item column: *Balance MAP*. This indicates that we are balancing our checkbook with our MAP. The numeral 2 in the (+) column indicates that our MAP balance was $2 less than our checkbook balance, and we have added $2 to the Miscellaneous money box to make the two accounts balance.

If the MAP total is *more* than your checkbook, *subtract* the difference from your Miscellaneous money box. If the difference is more than $5, you have probably made an error in recording somewhere. The simplest way to find the error is to go back through your checkbook and double-check each transfer of information from your checkbook to the MAP. This is another reason to update your MAP weekly—it's easier to find a mistake when you are reviewing twenty-five entries, compared to one hundred entries.

Use a New MAP Form Each Month

You will use a new MAP each month, transferring all the ending balances from last month's MAP to the BB (beginning balance) column of the current month's MAP.

All Income Goes into the Checkbook

Record 100 percent of your take-home income on your MAP. Do not cash a paycheck, put $100 in your pocket, and then deposit the rest in your checking account. Deposit the entire paycheck, and then if needed, write a check for $100 and cash it (or withdraw $100 in cash from the ATM—but remember to record the withdrawal in your checkbook register and on your MAP). When you update your MAP, account for that $100 in cash by recording it in the money box corresponding with how the cash will be spent (Husband Allowance or Wife Allowance, for example). By following this procedure, you will establish a clear paper trail to document your income and expense activities.

Pay All Expenses out of the Checkbook

Try to pay for everything by check with the exception of small personal allowance expenses. These should be paid for out of the personal allowance money you carry in your pocket or purse. This cash is the money you use for lunches, golf, movies, haircuts, and personal items.

Electronic Banking and the MAP

Our banking system is rapidly moving away from using paper checks—and even cash. Many people now pay all their bills on-line and seldom use checks. It is not uncommon for companies to use direct deposit for paychecks. You might be asking, "Will the MAP system work within this new electronic age?" *Absolutely.* It does not matter if your company makes a direct deposit or you make a regular trip to the bank to deposit your paycheck. Likewise, with payments it does not matter if you write a paper check or send an electronic check. The vehicle for receiving income or making payments is not the issue in using the MAP system. The key in making all this work is keeping good records and updating your MAP every week with your new income and expenses.

What about people who use credit cards to pay for practically everything and write just one check per month? Once again, no problem! The key is keeping track of all your charges, updating your MAP each week, and transferring money into your Credit Cards money box. The same is true for using an ATM or debit card. The MAP is a very simple and flexible money management system; it only requires that you keep good records and keep your MAP up to date.

While we are on the topic of credit cards, debit cards, and ATM transactions, let me make a suggestion. Every time you use one of these conveniences, put the receipt in the same location. For example, I always fold the receipt in half and put it in the middle section of my wallet. I don't put it in my shirt pocket, pants pocket, laptop computer bag, on the front seat of the car, or in the trash can. I always put receipts in one place—my wallet! That way I always know where to find them. Then, each week I pull out all the receipts and update my MAP. The key here is consistency and finding a place where receipts won't be misplaced, moved, or discarded by you or someone else.

Personal Allowances

Let me explain why it is so important for every MAP to have Personal Allowance money boxes. I can sum it up in one word: *Freedom!*

With the MAP system, you will not have to walk around with a $3'' \times 5''$ card in your pocket to record every penny you spend. With your personal allowance—which I recommend you carry as cash, for ultimate convenience—you are free to spend money on small things without having to record every dollar. Your personal allowance should be *a minimum of $50 to $100 per month for each spouse.* In my opinion, this is a minimum, nonnegotiable budget item. Everybody needs some personal money!

When you need personal allowance money, you should write a check and cash it at the bank. This cashed check is then recorded in the (−) column of the Personal Allowance money box on your MAP. If you have a large personal allowance expense, it is okay to write a check. This check will then be recorded in your Personal Allowance money box. For most small personal expenses, it will be easier to just pay cash. But remember, *always* write a check (paper or electronic) when you spend money for nonpersonal expenses such as groceries, monthly bills, clothing, and gifts. Writing a check establishes a paper trail for those expenditures and makes record keeping a lot easier. Also, as mentioned earlier, credit cards, electronic checks, and debit cards can also be used as long as you maintain a paper trail of your transactions.

On our sample MAP form, if you look at the Husband Allowance money box, you'll see that check number 507 was written for $50. This means that the husband went to the bank, cashed a check for $50, and put the money in his pocket. This money can now be spent for personal expenses during the week or month.

A Personal Note to Tightwads

When I reach this point in my seminar presentations, I typically take a few moments to get really personal with my audience. From my years of helping people with money management, I have realized that I must make a few comments to men or women who are tightwads. I have observed that some spouses like to keep a really "tight" budget. Everyone in the family is instructed to record every penny he or she spends on a 3″ × 5″ card to be turned in each day (or some variation of this plan).

If you're inclined to be a tightwad and a "tracker," loosen up! These plans very seldom work, especially if you demand that it be done *your* way. Give your spouse some freedom! Give *yourself* some freedom! The Personal Allowance money box is designed specifically to give husbands and wives the freedom to make their own spending choices. Don't fight over how every penny was or will be spent. In my opinion, tightwad budgets are one sure way to take all the fun out of a marriage.

Spend Based on the MAP Money Box, *Not* the Checkbook Balance

If you are operating according to a MAP, your checkbook balance will grow because you are allocating funds on a monthly basis for Christmas, car insurance premiums, and future things like vacations. *You must not spend based on the checkbook balance!* Base your spending on the balance in each individual money box category. Your checkbook balance is the sum of everything that has been allocated into your MAP money boxes. For specific purchases, you should spend according to what your MAP says you have available in the corresponding money box. You may have several thousand dollars in your checkbook balance, but if the balance in your Clothing money box is $200, you have only $200 available to spend on clothes. The rest of the money in your checkbook has already been allocated to other money boxes.

MAP Account "Paper Transfers"

You can do MAP money box transfers any time you like. For example, if you stop by the grocery store and do not have the checkbook but spend $20 of your personal allowance money, you can tuck the grocery receipt into your billfold or purse, and at the end of the week when you update the budget, simply transfer $20 from the Food money box to your Personal Allowance money box. Of course, the $20 you spend will not arrive back in your pocket until you cash a check, but the money will be back in your Personal Allowance money box and available for you to use.

For an example of this, look at the Food and Husband Allowance money boxes on the sample MAP form (see pages 96–97. You will that see $20 was taken out of the Food money box and $20 was put into the Husband Allowance money box.

When a Money Box Becomes a Minus

When you run out of money in a money box, stop spending money in that category. Remember, it's impossible to take money out of an empty box. However, if this does happen by mistake, simply decide which positive-balance money box you want to dip into to transfer funds and complete the transaction on your MAP form.

Please hear me loud and clear on this point: If you continually run negative balances on your MAP, you are wasting your time and the system has lost all its integrity. Thousands of people over the past fifteen years have found the MAP to be a great tool for managing their finances, but it is only a tool, and it takes commitment and discipline to make it work (just like anything in life that's worth doing). If you continually run negative balances on your MAP, you need to address the underlying issues and decide to bring your spending in line with your resources and your predetermined, prayed-about plan. It's just that simple. I want to encourage you to stay at the task, and don't give up if you stumble every now and then. If it would encourage you to know this, even I, Ethan Pope, the creator of the MAP, have done the impossible on occasion by taking money out of an empty money box. (I realize this may be hard for you to believe, but it's true.) If this happens to you, simply correct the problem and keep pressing on! There has only been one perfect person who ever walked the earth. It's not you, and it's surely not me.

Debt Repayment Money Box

If you have outstanding debts you are paying off monthly, not including your home or car, you should have a Debt Repayment money box on your MAP. This category would be used if you have outstanding credit card debt *when you first begin using the MAP*. Do not pay "old credit card debt" out of the Credit Cards money box. That category is reserved for *current* or *future* credit card use, and you will be paying each month's bill in full. If you have existing balances that you need to pay off, debt repayment should be part of your overall plan, and it should have its own money box.

Other items that might fall into the Debt Repayment category are "old" school loans, furniture or appliance loans, and medical bills that had not been paid off when you started using the MAP.

When you do your initial planning, you should allocate money into a Debt Repayment money box just like you would allocate money into the Food money box. Review the discussion of priorities in chapter 6 ("A Simple Financial Plan") for suggestions on how to pay off your debt. If you have debt, then debt repayment should be a high priority in your MAP budget.

Should I Keep All the MAP Money in a Checking Account?

The first rule for your checking account is to find one that pays interest. Then, after you have established your MAP, if your checking account balance is consistently more than the equivalent of one month's salary, you should transfer the surplus into a money market account where it will earn more interest than it would in your checking account. By using this plan, you are able to earn additional interest while having the money available for your use. Most money market accounts allow you to write *only* three to five checks per month, but some allow you to transfer funds between your checking and money market accounts several times each month.

When you need funds to pay for a large expense, such as an annual life insurance premium, Christmas gifts, or a semiannual car insurance premium, you simply transfer the necessary funds out of your money market account into your checking account. After the funds have been transferred, you can write the check out of your checkbook.

If you are using a checking account and a money market account, use the following formula to balance your budget:

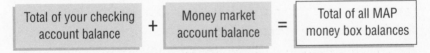

Figure 10-3

Notice that the total of your checking account plus the total of your money market account equals the total of all your MAP categories. There is no need to create or designate MAP money boxes to represent the balance in your money market account (for example, insurance, savings, or Christmas gifts). This would be too confusing and complicated. A money market account is simply a means for earning interest on lump sums of money that are not immediately needed for cash flow. Remember, the total of both accounts (checking and money market) will equal the total of all your MAP money boxes.

Investments

Except for short-term savings and emergency funds, investments are not tracked within the MAP system. You may have an Investment money box, where you will record your monthly installments, but once you write the check and make the investment, the transaction is completed, and the balance in your Investment money box would be zero. For example, if you are saving $250 each month for an IRA, these funds remain in the MAP until you write the check. On the sample MAP form in the Retirement (IRA) money box, you will notice we had a beginning balance of $750, to which we added our monthly deposit of $250, for a total of $1,000. We then wrote check 541 for $1,000 when we invested this money in an IRA, and the ending balance for the month is zero.

IRAs and other investments should be accounted for on a personal balance sheet. Savings for college, if kept in a mutual fund, would also be accounted for outside the MAP system. Investment money simply "flows through" the MAP—we record our budgeted amounts on the MAP, but later remove them from the system once the investment is purchased.

Accomplishing Our Three Objectives

By now I hope you can see how a MAP can help you become more

- Generous in your giving

- Consistent in your savings

- Free in your spending

On top of these three benefits, I trust you can also see how the MAP system helps you to exercise greater self-control and wisdom in all your financial transactions.

Guidelines for Starting Your First MAP

1. On the front page, fill out the first two columns, MAP Money Box and MAP Planned Amount, using your MAP Planning Worksheet as a guide. These columns are where you will list all your different money boxes and the monthly amount you plan to allocate into each one.

2. On the inside and back pages, fill in all the MAP money box headings, making sure that every category on the front page has a corresponding money box. So, you would designate a money box for Giving, Emergency Fund, IRA (if you have one), Mortgage, Electricity, and so on. Our sample form has thirty-one money boxes. Yours may have more or fewer, depending on your situation.

3. Next, determine the present balance in your check-book, and allocate the money into one or more money boxes inside your MAP. Do not record this amount on the front page of the MAP, because this is not a deposit. You are simply allocating the money that is already in your checking account. Let's say, for purposes of illustration, that your current checkbook balance is $500. You might choose to allocate $100 into Short-Term Savings, $100 into Car Repairs, $100 into your Personal Allowance, $100 into Gifts, and

$100 into Miscellaneous. It does not matter how the initial funds are distributed into the MAP money boxes. However, if you do not have an emergency fund, you might consider funding your Emergency Fund money box with your initial money.

4. When you are finished, the total of your checkbook balance should equal the total of all your MAP budget categories.

5. When you receive your next paycheck, you are ready to allocate your take-home pay into all of your money boxes, according to the allocation plan you worked out on your MAP Planning Worksheet and recorded on the front page of your MAP form.

6. Finally, begin using your MAP on a daily, weekly, and monthly basis to manage your finances, following the guidelines you have learned in this book.

Starting Your Own MAP

To create your MAP for the first time, you will need a blank MAP form. You will receive a special discount on a Start-up MAP Kit as a thank-you for purchasing this book.

To order your Start-up MAP Kit:

Visit our Web site
www.foundationsforliving.org

Write to
Ethan Pope
Foundations For Living
P.O. Box 15356
Hattiesburg, MS 39404

Or call
(601) 582-2000

Here's what you will receive:
- One-year supply of 8½″ × 11″ MAP forms
- Sample MAP Form
- MAP Planning Worksheets (sample and blank)
- Instructional cassette tape or CD

Be sure to use this special code when placing your order:
TYNMAP

Check out the special MAP area on our Web site for updated MAP information, MAP Q&A's, MAP money management tips, and MAP user testimonies.

CHAPTER ELEVEN

Common Budgeting Myths
Top Ten Reasons Why People Don't Budget

A MYTH IS SOMETHING THAT APPEARS TO BE TRUE BUT IN REALITY IS NOT. Some of the budgeting myths listed below might be true for some budgeting systems, but they are definitely not true for the MAP. One of your keys to successfully creating and using a MAP is to eliminate these common budgeting myths. Here are the top ten budgeting myths I have discovered in the past few years.

Myth #1: I don't have enough money to budget.

The Truth: People who have a limited income are the ones who need a budget the most. The fact is, wealthy people can afford to make some financial mistakes because they have more of a cushion. People who are living on a very limited income are the ones who need to plan the use of every dollar for maximum benefit. Every dollar that is not allocated has a great risk of being wasted or being spent on something that is really not a priority.

Myth #2: Budgets are too detailed and complex, and they take too much time.

The Truth: Some budgets are too complex—especially those that use a notebook with forty-five tabs (like my first budgeting system) and require several hours each week to keep it updated. However, the MAP is a simple plan: one sheet of paper per month and about thirty to forty-five minutes per week to update.

Myth #3: Budgets never work. I have tried and failed.

The Truth: Maybe you have been trying the wrong system. Most people quit because the budget is too confining or they have to spend too much time keeping it updated. The MAP system is simple to use and easy to maintain. Why not give it a try?

Myth #4: Budgets only cause arguments for couples.

The Truth: If properly used, a budget can *eliminate* arguments because it establishes a plan that both spouses agree upon before the next paycheck arrives. Remember, differing values in a marriage are what cause most arguments. With the MAP system and a biblical understanding of stewardship (God owns it all!), a couple is free to establish biblical priorities and values for how their entrusted resources will be used. Once the MAP has been created, the system is easy to follow. If there's money in a particular money box, you can spend it—no need to talk about it, pray about it, or fight about it. It's a done deal. Period. If a particular money box is empty, you can't spend any money in that category—no need to stomp your feet, cry, or scheme. It's that simple.

Budgets can bring true financial freedom to your family if you are using the right one. In fact, I am convinced that a family that plans how every dollar will be spent before it arrives will have the ability to have more fun and do more things than the family that does not budget.

Myth #5: Budgets are to be used to control your spouse.

The Truth: Budgets are never to be used to control or penalize your spouse. Budgets should be created together and used together. Husbands and wives should never take funds away from their spouse to punish them. This immature action on the part of one spouse would only give Satan an opportunity to use finances to destroy the marriage (see Ephesians 4:26-27). The goals of a MAP are to bring about better communication, more freedom, and less frustration.

Myth #6: I will start budgeting when I get married.

The Truth: If you don't budget when you're single, it is very likely that you will continue the same habits after you're married. But if you learn to live on a budget when you're single, you and your spouse will very likely live on a budget and reap the benefits as a couple.

Myth #7: I don't have the personality to budget.

The Truth: What a cop-out! Personality has very little to do with budgeting. More likely, what these folks are lacking is *self-discipline*. Laziness comes in all shapes, sizes, and colors.

Myth #8: I only need to update my budget once a month.

The Truth: If you only update your budget once a month, you're not managing your finances, you're simply tracking where the money was spent. If you update your MAP weekly, it will help you to make good spending decisions and keep you out of financial trouble.

Myth #9: My spouse does not want to live on a budget.

The Truth: This is one of the most valid reasons why a budget might not work in your marriage. I will be the first to agree that in a marriage it takes both the husband and wife in agreement to plan and use a budget. If your spouse is not willing to use a MAP, let me give you several suggestions: (1) pray; (2) ask him or her to read this book; (3) be honest about your frustration in the area of money; and (4) ask him or her to give the simple MAP system a test drive for six months.

Myth #10: I plan to start budgeting next year.

The Truth: How many times have you said this before? Now is the best time to begin using a MAP. You will always have an excuse for why you should start later or next year.

Most myths are simply weak excuses for being lazy. Here's the good news: You can get rid of this kind of thinking and begin making the right decisions today. If you are weak in this area, ask God to give you strength.

CHAPTER TWELVE

Solving Money Conflicts in Marriage
Learning to Negotiate Solutions

IF YOU ARE MARRIED, THE FIRST REAL CHALLENGE YOU MAY ENCOUNTER in creating your MAP may be your *spouse*. I am sure this is no surprise. When it comes to setting financial priorities and allocating your God-given resources, you may find that the person you love most, the one to whom you have committed your life, the one with whom you share everything—including the checkbook—has become a thorn in your side.

Now what am I supposed to do? Ethan, I thought you said something about more fun and less fights! What do we do when we simply cannot agree?

Some couples have told me, "It is impossible for us to agree on how our money should be allocated. All this system has done is create more stress and more arguments." For many couples, the MAP Planning Worksheet was only completed with many tears, a lot of prayer, and God's help. While you might prefer to avoid the tears, there's nothing wrong with investing a lot of prayer and needing God's help to get your financial life in order. We all need to learn God's principles for oneness, how to communicate more effectively in marriage, and how to negotiate solutions when we disagree with our spouse.

Here are some suggestions to help you break the gridlock:

Begin with prayer. Ask God to show you what to do. Ask him to reveal any selfish attitudes that are not honoring to him. Pray about your finances for a few days before you discuss the topic again. "If you need wisdom—if you want to know what God wants you to do—ask him, and he will gladly tell you" (James 1:5).

Listen, listen, and listen some more. Try to understand what your spouse is saying—not what you think he or she is saying but what is really being said. Value his or her perspective. Be quick to listen and slow to respond. "My dear brothers and sisters, be quick to listen, slow to speak, and slow to get angry" (James 1:19). Don't be mentally "building your case" while your spouse is talking. Listen! I mean really listen hard. Listen so well that you could repeat back what was said word for word if you had to. Give your spouse an opportunity to present his or her feelings without interruption—without your saying one word. Begin the conversation by saying something like this: "Honey, you talk as long as you need to share your heart. I will not say one word until you tell me that you are finished." I have learned that that has helped Janet to communicate what is on her heart without having to respond to all my questions or objections. When it's my turn, she gives me the same freedom to speak without interruptions.

Be spiritual. Don't act like a husband and wife who do not have a relationship with Jesus Christ. The deeds of the flesh are strife, jealousy, outbursts of anger, disputes, dissensions, factions, and envying, just to name a few (see Galatians 5:20-21). Is this how you should be treating your spouse? Wouldn't you rather exhibit the fruit of the Spirit, showing "love, joy, peace, patience, kindness, goodness, faithfulness, gentleness, and self-control" (Galatians 5:22-23)? Let these character qualities be your goal as you discuss your financial life.

Realize that your spouse is not your enemy. Your husband or wife should be your best friend, and you should treat each other that way. Satan is our real enemy, but sometimes we get confused and think that our spouse is the enemy. Satan is out to destroy your marriage, and one of his favorite tools is sowing discord about finances.

Initially, it might appear that developing your personal MAP is creating more problems than it is solving. However, I have found that most of the problems fade away once the MAP has been implemented. Let there be harmony and peace within your marriage. Please, don't give up on your spouse. Pray hard, listen hard, be spiritual, and recognize your common enemy! Don't give up on the MAP system. Most importantly, don't give up on God.

CHAPTER THIRTEEN

Roads to Avoid
Seven Common Problems

WHAT IF YOU WERE PLANNING A TRIP AND YOU FOUND OUT THAT I COULD
tell you, based on my own experience and that of others, all
the bad roads, horrible restaurants, and fleabag hotels to
avoid. Would you listen? Or would you choose to make your
own plans and do it your own way? Over the years, I have
seen several common problems occur repeatedly as people
start to use the MAP. If you'll heed my advice, however, you
can avoid most or all of these "potholes."

Pothole #1: Negative balances in several money boxes.

One woman called in to a radio program on which I was the
guest and said, "I always have numerous negative balances in
my budget. I just can't seem to keep things under control.
What should I do?" If certain money boxes always seem to
have a negative balance, ask yourself these two questions:
"Am I allocating enough money into these categories each
month?" or "Am I simply overspending due to a lack of discipline?"

If you truly are not allocating enough money into a particular money box, you will need to decrease your allocation to
another money box in order to increase the one that is short.
However, if you determine that you are already allocating adequate funds to each money box, the issue comes down to discipline. You must develop the discipline to stop spending
more than you have allocated! Remember, if there's no money
in the money box, you cannot go spend it!

If on a regular basis you have negative balances in several categories, your MAP has lost its integrity. If you cannot find the discipline to stop overspending, you might as well toss your MAP in the trash. Remember, the MAP is a tool, but it takes commitment and self-discipline for the tool to be effective.

Pothole # 2: My Miscellaneous money box is always in the negative.

A common problem for new MAP users is that they don't allocate enough each month into their Miscellaneous money box. Every MAP must have a Miscellaneous money box for occasional purchases such as film development and postage stamps, but miscellaneous expenses can be deadly for your MAP. Don't let this be true for you. Think through the kinds of things you will need to pay for out of your Miscellaneous money box and plan accordingly. Whatever you do, don't try to create a separate money box for every little thing. If you do, you'll end up with 120 different MAP categories. Unfortunately, some people actually try to do this. Save yourself the trouble; use a Miscellaneous money box for all the little things you need to spend money on.

How can we avoid this? The best advice is to carefully plan the allocation amount for this area of your MAP. Spend some time developing a list of all the once-in-a-while things you buy, such as postage stamps, Christmas cards, film, printer ink, home office supplies, storage boxes, shipping, just to name a few. Because each family is unique, I do not think it would be wise to suggest a specific dollar amount or percent. Remember, you can always adjust your allocation when you update your MAP. The purpose of the Miscellaneous money box is to keep your MAP simple by catching all the little things so you don't end up with 120 money boxes on your MAP!

Pothole # 3: Planning for annual or semiannual expenses.

Be sure to plan properly for annual or semiannual expenses, such as insurance premiums, property tax, and Christmas gifts. The problem is not the simple math ($1,200 per year ÷ 12 = $100 per month); the problem is that we forget to accrue for the annual expense. The MAP Planning Worksheet will help you plan properly for these expenses that you might otherwise forget.

If you don't have twelve months to save up for an annual expense, you will need to calculate how many months you have until you'll need the money and plan accordingly. For example, if you need $1,200 in 8 months, you would allocate $150 per month into the corresponding money box ($1,200 ÷ 8 = $150). After you have paid for the item and you have twelve months until you need the money again, you would adjust your allocation and begin to allocate $100 each month ($1,200 ÷ 12 = $100).

Pothole # 4: No emergency fund.

Every MAP must have an Emergency money box. This money is to be used when a crisis arises, such as an unexpected car repair bill that goes beyond what you have available to spend out of the Car Repairs money box. For example, if you have $500 in car repairs but only $300 in your Car Repairs money box, you would transfer $200 from your Emergency money box to your Car Repairs money box to make up the shortfall.

Once you have used a portion of your emergency fund to cover a shortfall in another money box, you must replenish the money you took out of your Emergency money box to bring your emergency fund back up to its budgeted level. How do we go about accomplishing this goal? If you are following the simple financial plan outlined in chapter 6, your emergency fund allocation will be either 3 percent of your monthly take-home pay (Priority 2) or equal to one month's take-home pay (Priority 5). If you have completed Priority 2 (establishing your emergency fund) but have not yet reached Priority 5 (expanding your emergency fund), you will be focused on either paying off credit card debt and other consumer debt (Priority 3) or paying off your car loans (Priority 4).

Here's what you do: Simply decrease the amount you are allocating to pay off your credit cards or car and allocate those funds to replenish your minimum emergency fund (Priority 2) as rapidly as possible. Once your Emergency money box balance is back to its budgeted level, resume your plan to pay off your other debts.

If you have already expanded your emergency fund (Priority 5), you would decrease the amount you are saving or investing (Priority 6) or decrease the amount you are using to pay off your mortgage (Priority 7) until your expanded emergency fund balance once again equals one month's take-home pay.

The underlying principle is simple: Do not proceed to the next priority until all higher priorities have been accomplished. If, as in the case of our emergency fund, the fund is depleted due to an emergency, reallocate the necessary funds from lower priorities until the higher priority (emergency fund) is once again fulfilled.

Pothole # 5: No Personal Allowance money boxes.

As I have said in previous chapters, you must have a personal allowance. This money helps you to have some freedom in your budget. We all need some money we can spend without having to account for every dollar. When I go to the bank and cash a check to take money out of my Personal Allowance money box, I put the money in my wallet and spend it however I choose. I do not write down how much I spend for lunch or for anything else I buy with that money!

Pothole # 6: Forgetting to update the MAP each week.

My advice is to set aside a specific time each week to update your MAP. Get out your weekly calendar and write it down. If it's scheduled, it's more likely to get done. If you do this for several weeks or months, you will develop a habit. After Janet and I created our personal MAP, I developed the habit of sitting down every Friday night to update our MAP. Find the time that is most convenient for you, but make sure it's weekly so you don't lose control of your MAP.

Pothole # 7: Low Income.

If your take-home pay is consistently lower than what you are budgeting, you have only two options: Increase your income or cut
your expenses. You cannot continue to budget more than is actually coming into your checking account. It doesn't work.

A Final Word

These are some of the most common problems for new MAP users.
But I hope you can see how these potholes can be avoided by good
planning, following the guidelines of the MAP system, and practic-
ing self-control and wisdom. In the next chapter, I will address
another problem that some people have in using a MAP—that is,
living on commission.

CHAPTER FOURTEEN

Living on Commission
Adapting the MAP to Work for You

WHAT IF YOU'RE PAID ON COMMISSION OR DON'T RECEIVE THE SAME income every month? Will the MAP work for you? Absolutely! Here's how you can do it: Base your MAP on your *average* monthly income. During months when you have an income surplus, put it into your Short-Term Savings money box. During months when you have an income shortfall, withdraw the amount you need from the same Short-Term Savings money box.

For anyone, discipline is the key to successful budgeting. This is especially true when your income fluctuates from month to month. When your monthly income is high, you must be diligent to set aside a portion of that income to supplement your income in lower-income months. *The goal is to maintain a consistent lifestyle from month to month.*

Let's take a closer look at how you would do this.

The first thing to do is determine your average monthly income for the past twelve months. For purposes of illustration, let's assume we have received the following paychecks for the past year:

January	$6,000	August	$4,800
February	$4,000	September	$8,000
March	$5,000	October	$4,000
April	$2,000	November	$1,000
May	$3,000	December	$4,400
June	$3,400	**Total Income**	**$51,000**
July	$5,400		

The monthly average equals total income divided by twelve months ($51,000 ÷ 12 = $4,250 per month). To be conservative, I would recommend that this family budget their giving, saving, and spending based on $4,000 per month. To be clear, this family's total monthly MAP allocation would equal $4,000. I strongly suggest that you be very conservative with your monthly MAP allocations when you're operating on an inconsistent income. It is much easier to deal with a surplus each month than a shortfall.

The graph below shows why an inconsistent lifestyle can easily lead to stress and depression when actual income drops below budgeted income. One month you're eating steak and lobster, the next month it's bread and water.

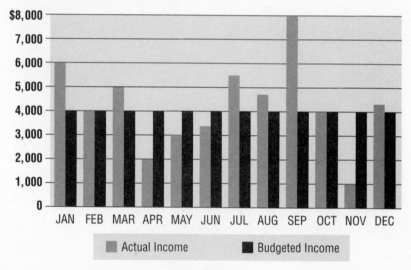

Figure 14-1

Establish a MAP Money Box (Flex Income) for the Surplus

In order for this plan to work, I suggest that you establish a MAP money box to store your surplus income each month and to take money from when you have a shortfall. Using our sample MAP form balance of $4,000 per month as an example, when more than $4,000 is received in a month, we would faithfully allocate the excess earnings for the month into our Flex Income money box. In a month when less than $4,000 is received during the month, we would calculate the shortfall and transfer money *out* of our Flex Income money box into the one or more MAP money boxes that did not receive allocations from our paycheck.

The following chart shows how this system would work over the span of twelve months when income varies from month to month.

MONTH	ACTUAL INCOME RECEIVED	DOLLARS ADDED TO FLEX INCOME MONEY BOX	DOLLARS TAKEN OUT OF FLEX INCOME MONEY BOX	BALANCE OF FLEX INCOME MONEY BOX	TOTAL OF MONTHLY MAP ALLOCATIONS
January	$5,000	$1,000	0	$1,000	$4,000
February	4,000	0	0	1,000	4,000
March	6,000	2,000	0	3,000	4,000
April	3,000	0	1,000	2,000	4,000
May	2,000	0	2,000	0	4,000
June	5,000	1,000	0	1,000	4,000
July	5,000	1,000	0	2,000	4,000
August	4,500	500	0	2,500	4,000
September	6,000	2,000	0	4,500	4,000
October	1,000	0	3,000	1,500	4,000
November	4,000	0	0	1,500	4,000
December	3,000	0	1,000	500	4,000

Figure 14-2

Actual Income Received

This column represents the total of all the income you have received and have available to allocate this month. This could simply be the amount of one paycheck if you receive only one paycheck each month. Or this amount could be the total of several paychecks, plus any other income you received. In very simple terms, "How much income did you receive this month?"

Dollars Added to Flex Income Money Box

Determine this figure by taking the income for the month and subtracting the planned budget amount. For January in our example, this would be $5,000 income – $4,000 budgeted = $1,000 surplus.

Dollars Taken Out of Flex Income Money Box

Determine this figure by subtracting your income for the month from the planned budget amount. This will be the amount of money you will transfer out of your Flex Income money box and into other money boxes that did not receive funding this month. For April in our example, this would be $4,000 budgeted – $3,000 income = $1,000 shortfall.

Balance of Flex Income Money Box

The current balance in the Flex Income money box each month is shown in this column. These are the funds available to be transferred into other MAP money boxes when your monthly income is less than the budgeted amount on your MAP.

Total of Monthly MAP Allocations

The total in this column will always equal your total monthly MAP budget. It should also equal either the *difference* between the Actual Income Received column and the Dollars Added to Flex Income Money Box column, or the *sum* of the Actual Income Received column and Dollars Taken Out of Flex Income Money Box column.

What if your monthly income is less than your MAP balance, and you don't have any money in your Flex Income money box?

If you don't have any money set aside to cover a shortfall, you have only one option: Allocate exactly what came in. This may require some tough choices as you allocate funds among your MAP money boxes. Your first priority will be to allocate money for all your fixed expenses, such as your mortgage or rent and utilities. Then, allocate the remaining funds into the other MAP money boxes. If the shortfall continues for more than three months, *reduce* your planned budget allocations until your circumstances change. *Do not use debt to live beyond your means.*

I encourage you to be a faithful steward of the resources that God has entrusted to you at this time. It is better to be realistic and lower your standard of living than to foolishly keep living at a level of income you are not presently earning. If and when your income increases, *then* you have the freedom to increase your budget allocations.

CHAPTER FIFTEEN

What Should We Do . . . ?

Common Questions about the MAP

Q: I've tried different budgeting systems. What makes the MAP system different?

A: First of all, it's simple, it's unique, and it offers a fresh approach to budgeting. Most budgeting systems fail because they are far too complicated, they don't address the biblical basis of stewardship, they don't address our attitudes toward money, and they are not based on easy-to-understand money management principles.

The MAP system is more than just a budgeting system. It begins with foundational biblical principles, such as "God owns it all" and "We must be faithful stewards." It includes helpful "attitude" concepts, such as "It's impossible to take money out of an empty box." The MAP system is also more than just an accounting system—it is a way of life. Moreover, the MAP system is different because it is simple. Just think about it. It operates on one sheet of paper each month, and it takes most families about thirty minutes to update each week.

With the MAP system, you determine ahead of time where the money is going to be allocated—then you help each dollar arrive at its predetermined destination.

Q: What do I do when my spouse does not want to use a MAP?

A: Begin by praying. Ask God to change his or her heart. I have found in many cases that the real problem is spiritual. Some spouses simply do not want to have any spending guidelines. They want to buy what they want, when they want it. God needs to change their heart. Ask your spouse to read this book, and maybe God will change his or her attitude. Most people who do not want to budget are afraid to try because of past failures, or they don't want to be told what they can and cannot do. Finally, you could go through one of our Bible studies with your spouse. For more information and other resources, go to our Web site: www.foundationsforliving.org

Q: Our income is not enough to cover our expenses. What can we do?

A: In simple terms, you have only two options: Decrease your expenses or increase your income. Which one is easier for you? You cannot allow your expenses to exceed your income month after month. You must make some changes. Can you find a less expensive place to live? Can you work a second job? Do what it takes to bring your expenses in line with your income. If you continue to live beyond your means, you will inevitably have a financial crisis. I guarantee it!

Q: Do we have to use one checkbook with your system?

A: I recommend that you use one checkbook, because it makes things simpler. However, if each spouse wants to have a checkbook, just make sure to balance your MAP each week by adding the two checkbook balances together, which should equal the total of all your MAP money box allocations. If you are using credit cards, ATM cards, or debit cards for convenience, as we discussed in an earlier chapter, agree with your spouse to keep all receipts in a consistent location so they are not misplaced, moved, or discarded.

Q: Who should update the MAP? The husband or wife?

A: I believe that the best system is for husbands and wives to take turns updating the MAP each week. There is nothing better than hands-on experience. Direct involvement will also help each spouse to have a better understanding of the MAP system. If one spouse is simply not an administrator, the other spouse can keep the MAP updated each week. However, no matter who actually updates the MAP each week, both spouses need to look at the MAP before spending money to see how much is remaining in each MAP money box.

Q: My kids keep overspending (for example, on cell phones and gas for the car). What should I do?

A: Who is in charge? You or the kids? The answer is simple. Take the cell phone or car away for a few weeks! No, I am not kidding. Children need to learn that there are limits or they will grow up to be adults who squander their resources. Demonstrate tough love when necessary. One of your goals as a parent is to prepare your children to become responsible adults. Don't neglect your responsibility.

Q: What if we keep having negative balances in numerous categories. What should we do?

A: First of all, you are to be congratulated for accomplishing the impossible: You have been able to take money out of an empty box! All jokes aside, I realize that on occasion you might go to the store without looking at your MAP, write a check for an item, come home to record it on your MAP, and discover that you have no money to spend in that specific money box.

If this is a rare exception, no problem. Simply transfer money from another money box. However, if this overspending continues month after month and has become a lifestyle, I strongly urge you to change your habits. Otherwise, you might as well take your MAP form, wad it up into a big ball, and throw it into the trash can.

Q: What do you think about computer budgeting programs?

A: Some people love to use computer programs, but I have been surprised at how many people have told me they prefer the manual MAP system. They say it is easier, and they like it that way. It's very easy to pull out the MAP form and glance over it before they walk out the door to go shopping. No need to turn on the computer, load up the program, and wait. However, if you prefer computer software, I encourage you to periodically check our Web site, www.foundationsforliving.org. We hope to offer MAP software at some point in the future.

Q: My spouse and I are always fighting about money, and the stress is just too much. What can we do?

A: There are probably two main reasons you are always fighting about money: (1) You have differing values, and/or (2) you have not yet created a personal MAP for your finances. For most couples, creating a MAP increases communication about values and reduces stress and arguments. Because the MAP system is so simple and straightforward (if there is money in a specific money box, you can either spend it or leave it), when the time comes to go shopping, there's no need to pray about it, discuss it, or fight about it. Using a MAP will really simplify your life.

Q: Why do I need to update the MAP each week? I would rather do it once a month.

A: If you update your MAP at the end of each month, all you are doing is tracking where you spent the money. In my opinion, that is a complete waste of time. We update the MAP each week because the MAP system has a higher priority—to help you look to the future and plan your spending. The MAP is designed to help you make spending decisions today, tomorrow, and next week—not just track what you have already spent. A MAP will help you keep your spending under control. If you do not update your MAP each week, you could spend more than you planned but not realize it until it's too late. Weekly updates are one of the core ingredients of a successful MAP system.

Q: What does the Bible teach about budgeting?

A: The Bible is full of principles that apply to budgeting. These principles are discussed in chapter 4 ("Budgetology"), where we establish a biblical foundation for budgeting. A proper theology of budgeting begins with the truths that God owns everything, we are stewards, and we are called to be faithful. "Know the state of your flocks, and put your heart into caring for your herds, for riches don't last forever, and the crown might not be secure for the next generation. After the hay is harvested, the new crop appears, and the mountain grasses are gathered in, your sheep will provide wool for clothing, and your goats will be sold for the price of a field. And you will have enough goats' milk for you, your family, and your servants" (Proverbs 27:23-27). In other words, if you carefully manage your possessions, you will have money for food, shelter, and clothing.

Q: I cannot control my spending, and this has destroyed every budget I have ever tried to establish. I know that I am very materialistic. Please help me. How can I change?

A: First question: Have you surrendered your life to Christ? As Jesus told Nicodemus in John 3:7, "You must be born again." A person whose life has not been surrendered to Christ is more likely to overspend simply because the person is not living according to godly principles. Second Corinthians 5:17 says, "Therefore if any man is in Christ, he is a new creature; the old things passed away; behold, new things have come" (NASB). Also, Galatians 5:22 tells us, "When the Holy Spirit controls our lives, he will produce this kind of fruit in us: love, joy, peace, patience, kindness, goodness, faithfulness, gentleness, and *self-control*" (emphasis added).

Ask God to give you the power to control your spending. And stop putting yourself in situations where you are tempted to overspend. Also, I recommend that you find an accountability partner who will check in with you each week to be certain you are following your MAP and not overspending.

Visit the Foundations for Living Web site for links to articles and spiritual help in this area.

Q: How can a "spender" change?

A: In most cases, spenders become savers when they grow tired of living on the edge and when they become disgusted with credit card bills they cannot pay.

Q: I am having a hard time forgiving my spouse for putting us into a financial mess. What should I do?

A: Look at it this way: God wants you to forgive your spouse, and Satan wants you to be at odds with your spouse for the rest of your life. Satan knows that without forgiveness, there is a greater possibility your marriage will end in divorce. We're all sinners in need of forgiveness. Ask God to give you the grace you need to forgive your spouse. As hard as it is, ask God to use this for good in your marriage. Don't allow Satan the victory; forgive your spouse today. If you need help, I encourage you to talk with your pastor or a marriage counselor.

Q: Is it okay for spouses to maintain separate budgets?

A: You are living in the danger zone with this one. Be careful. A "his and hers" philosophy of money management does not bring about unity or oneness in marriage. Instead, it promotes separation and self-centeredness. Also, remember that it is not *my* money or *your* money; it's all *God's* money. Part of God's plan for marriage is that husbands and wives do things *together*—dream together, pray together, give together, raise a family together, cry together, laugh together, and yes, even budget your money together. Ever since the beginning, God's plan has been for oneness in marriage—and your marriage is no exception.

Also, don't forget that Personal Allowance money boxes are an important part of the MAP system. These money boxes allow husbands and wives to spend some money however they choose each month.

Q: What if I just don't want to budget? What would you say to me?

A: Grow up. We're stewards of God's resources, whether we recognize it or not. The MAP system simply helps us to be wise and faithful stewards.

Q: What is the best way to save money?

A: Many people have learned that the easiest way to save money is through a payroll deduction plan, where the money is taken out before they even see it. Check with your employer to see if this option is available.

Q: Giving has always been a struggle. How can you help?

A: When giving becomes a real value or priority in your life, you will be willing to make the necessary lifestyle changes to make it a reality. We typically do what we really want to do. If you *really* want to give, you'll find a way to make it happen.

Q: What is the key to budgeting success?

A: Simple. Self-control. It also helps to have a simple plan for allocating the resources you have available. Naturally, I recommend the MAP system.

Q: I sense my values are all messed up. How do I go about changing my core values?

A: Read God's Word on a daily basis. Study God's Word. Meditate on God's Word. Memorize God's Word (I encourage you to start with Psalm 1). Pray. Commit yourself to accountable relationships with godly people.

Q: When should children start using a MAP?

A: Whenever they start asking for money. Depending on their age, you may not expect them to use a MAP form. Instead, give them three jars: one for giving, one for saving, and one for spending. Teach them how to allocate their money into the jars, and teach them that when a jar is empty, there is no more money to spend. See appendix B for more information on teaching children to use the MAP.

Q: My financial life is a mess. Is there hope for me?

A: As long as you are still breathing, there's hope. Ask God to change your heart today. Forget what lies behind, and press on toward the future. If your financial life is a mess, it is probably because you have not been living on a Money Allocation Plan. Create a MAP, and develop the discipline to live by it. You can turn your life around with prayer, planning, and God's grace.

Visit our Web site (www.foundationsforliving.org) for answers to more questions on financial topics. If you have a question you want to ask Ethan Pope, send him an e-mail (info@foundationsforliving.org).

CHAPTER SIXTEEN

Decision Time
Putting What You've Learned into Action

IT HAS BEEN GREAT TO TRAVEL A FEW MILES DOWN THE ROAD OF LIFE WITH you on your journey through this book. I am confident that as you have turned the pages, you've said, "Now that makes sense" or "I've never understood that before." It's possible you've laughed, or maybe you've cried. Perhaps you've shouted out "Yes!" On occasion, you may have disagreed with something I've said. However, now that you've reached the end of the book, it's time to put what you've learned into action.

The goal of this book is for you to actually create and use your own personal MAP. Now comes the hard part—doing it. I realize it can be difficult to make changes in your life, but I also know that the benefits of using the MAP are well worth the effort. I know that the world is doing everything in its power to squeeze you into its mold (see Romans 12:1-2). However, we don't live in the world's economy, we live in God's economy. We don't live with a temporal perspective, we live with an eternal perspective. We don't make our decisions based on what the world says, we make our decisions based upon a Christian worldview. "See to it that no one takes you captive through philosophy and empty deception, according to the tradition of men, according to the elementary principles of the world, rather than according to Christ" (Colossians 2:8, NASB).

My challenge to you is to finish strong what you have begun so that when you stand before the Lord to give an account of your life, you will hear the words, "Well done, my good and faithful steward."

For your convenience, here's a summary of the major points of MAP making:

- God owns it all; therefore, we are stewards.

- It is required of stewards to be faithful.

- God cares about how we manage 100 percent of his resources, not just what we give.

- How we give, save, and spend our money reflects our values.

- Plan your MAP allocations *before* the paycheck arrives—not while you are shopping.

- Every dollar has a destination. You determine ahead of time where the money will be allocated—then you help each dollar arrive at its predetermined destination.

- When there is money in a MAP money box, you can either spend it or leave it.

- When there is no money in a MAP box, you cannot spend it.

- It's impossible to take money out of an empty box.

- Satan is doing everything in his power to have you take a spiritual and financial detour in life. Recognize that Satan—not your spouse—is your enemy.

- Every person should pursue a goal to become 100 percent debt free at some point in life.

- The MAP operates on a single sheet of paper every month.

- The MAP takes a big-picture approach—no 3″ × 5″ cards, no tracking every dime you spend.

- The MAP looks to the future instead of focusing on where the money went.

- The MAP uses take-home pay.

- Don't allow a money box to have a negative balance.

- Most money problems arise out of differing values, not the amount of money you are earning.

- MAPs are simple to use.

- MAPs help you to be generous in your giving, consistent in your saving, and free in your spending.

As I said in the introduction, a MAP can alleviate stress, save your marriage, help you to pay all your credit card bills in full every month, accelerate paying off your mortgage, put you on a path to becoming 100 percent debt free, allow you to generously support God's kingdom financially, and help you to be a faithful steward of God's resources. As I write the final lines of this chapter, I am more convinced than ever of the truth of these words.

Now it's *decision time*. Life is too short and eternity is too long not to make the right decisions today. Press on, my friend, toward the goal of wise financial stewardship. You can do it!

On the following pages, you will read the personal testimonies of a few MAP users from across the nation. I pray that God will use their experiences with the MAP as an encouragement in your life.

CHAPTER SEVENTEEN

"I Love These Things!"
MAP Users Speak Out

SINCE 1995, I HAVE RECEIVED THOUSANDS OF LETTERS FROM PEOPLE WHO have heard me on the radio, attended one of my seminars, or read one of my books. Over the years, I have tucked some of these encouraging letters into a special file in my office. In this chapter, you will hear from some of these people. All of them are MAP users and have been for years. All but two wrote to me unsolicited to share how the MAP system has helped them to stop living from paycheck to paycheck, removed stress in their marriage, helped them get out of debt, taught them how to save money, encouraged them to pay their credit card bills in full each month, and simply to have more fun, less fights.

If others can be successful using the MAP, so can you. I pray that these letters will be an encouragement to you.

Monica from Mississippi:

"We came to a seminar of yours at the end of 1993. We started using your MAP plan and the financial principles we learned at the first of 1994. You were right, the first one went into the trash can—but we continued on the next month and the next, and even now with the plan. As the debts melted away, so did our financial worries. What a difference you made in our lives! Thank you for that. It was great to hear you on a Christian radio program and to know that these godly principles of managing money were being made available to all who would listen. We are witnesses to the fact that it is not always how much money you make . . . but how you use what you've got. We are not totally debt free—we have about six years on our mortgage—but we have come a long way with a new mindset, which is that we don't always have to be in debt and owe someone. Thank you very much for the difference that came into our lives, and may God continue to bless your ministry."

Neale from North Carolina:

"You can't know how deeply I appreciate you. I meant to tell you on the phone that you're the first man in my life that instructed me in healthy financial living. No one ever taught me the importance of saving, giving, and budgeting until you did back in Dallas. Most of what we have saved is a result of your investment in us. Thank you again."

Cecil from Texas:

"Thank you for putting us on the right financial footing with your budgeting (MAP) system years ago. The key thing we learned from you was to deduct credit card purchases from the appropriate money box when you make the purchase and transfer that amount to the Credit Card money box so you can pay that bill in full each month. Our only debts now are the car loan and the house. We've got the mortgage down to a fifteen-year loan now and will work on your idea for paying for a car next. Thanks for all the financial freedom."

Thelma from Michigan:

"Just a little note to let you know how much your book has revolutionized our lives in just two short months. I heard you on the Moody Radio Network, I believe about a year ago. I was driving my car, and I pulled off the road and wrote down your name and address. A few months later I looked up the address from my notes and ordered your book. When I got it, I glanced through it a little and thought, *This looks complicated, just like all the other books on money.* I just ignored it for months until about eight months later while counseling with our pastor on money matters—he insisted we start a budget. We

are in our mid-sixties and never had a bona fide budget in our lives! I
didn't think our pastor's method would work well for us, so I dug out
your book and started reading. What a pleasant surprise. The more I
read, the more excited I got. Within a couple of weeks we had our
budget (MAP) set up and working. Wow! What a change! We began
to see all kinds of ways to save money, and also holes where the
money was disappearing. Within a couple of weeks we had a balance
of at least $400 at all times in our checkbook. I told my husband we
probably will never again bounce a check. We had always been living
on the edge, with many times a minus balance in our checkbook, and
just getting a deposit in the nick of time—and once in a while not in
time, so we'd have an overdraft fine. And if we made a mistake, it
was really scary. That's all done now. Our bills are paid on time, so
no late fees; we have money in our checkbook, so no service fees. We
also opened up two savings accounts and will soon open up an inter-
est-bearing checking account. God bless you."

Terry from Arizona:
"Hi! Please send a one-year supply of MAP forms to me. I love
these things! God bless you all. Thanks."

Tim from Mississippi:
"Seven years ago I was in desperate need of the MAP system. My
wife and I were college students who had recently married and I
had begun working as a youth minister. My first church was paying me $5,000 a year and supplied a small house for us to live in.
My wife had a work-study job at the college, paying minimum
wage. I still wonder how we made it. Actually, we almost didn't. I
remember balancing the checkbook one day and there was $2 left,
and more bills to pay. I knew we needed help! We tried another system at first, but it was so complicated that I felt like it was controlling our lives rather than being a tool for us to control our finances.

"One day my pastor mentioned some resources he had used from
you. As soon as I understood the concepts involved, I knew that this

was the financial plan for us. It was simple and compact, two things the previous plan I had tried lacked. I drove to your office as soon as I could, picked up a year's supply of the MAP sheets, and we have been using them ever since. It is the best money I spend every year.

"One of the best things about the MAP plan is that it has been very adaptable to our different needs as our income and expenditures have changed. Two years ago, our son was born, and my wife stopped working outside the home to take care of him. Many of our friends of similar age and income have not been able to do this, so I am grateful that God has made this possible for us. I believe that using the MAP program to keep our finances under control was a major boost in our effort to plan and accomplish living off of one income when my wife stopped working in order to be at home full-time. Thanks again."

Billy from Georgia:
"Thank you so much for the very helpful tape and MAP sheets. When I first looked at them, I thought they were very complicated. However, the tape explained things very well. I know that the MAP will indeed lead to more fun and less fights."

Kelly from Ohio:
"It has been a full year now since I began the MAP system, and I have to tell you what a big difference it has made to my husband and me. I have quit running up the credit card bills and we have paid them all off. Our checking account balance no longer goes down to pennies or less. We have money waiting to pay the bills when they arrive. The best part is that the stress is gone—and so are the arguments. Thank you so much."

Debbie from New Jersey:
"I am so thankful for your ministry. I use the MAP forms every month and am happily debt free. I'm currently saving to buy a home."

Louis from Canada:

"My finances before using Ethan's Money Allocation Plan were chaotic. Although I am very analytical by nature and kept my checkbook balanced to the cent, I was absolutely incapable of income planning. Large, one-time expenses, such as tuition, meal plans, car insurance, etc., threw my finances into chaos. As a single man, my lifestyle was one of feast or famine.

"I knew how much money was in my account at all times. I could pay my credit card bill in full each month, although I struggled to get by toward the end of the month. After paying off the credit card bill, I had very little left to live on for the rest of the month. I had become so dependent, I had to use that credit card to survive!

"I was spending more than I made, so I also used student loans to supplement my income as a graduate student. I never questioned getting the loans (nor did I read the papers)—it was the thing to do. All my friends were doing this. I, like them, figured to repay these loans when I graduated and was making "big money." One last and most unfortunate characteristic of my life before MAPs: I did not tithe and gave very little.

"My need for better financial control crystallized when my wife and I announced our engagement. We had very different views on money: I was the spender, she was the saver. We were looking for common ground to resolve our financial differences. We learned that financial problems are a leading factor in marriages ending in divorce. That really scared me. I did not want money, and my mismanagement of it, to cause any harm to our marriage. We enrolled in Ethan's 'Smart Money Manager' course and learned about MAPs and a whole bunch more. We both agreed to change our habits and try things according to Ethan's suggestions.

"After almost three years of living on MAPs, all I can say is, Amazing! I can't believe how much more I am doing with the same amount of money, and the degree of control God has provided me over finances. I am so thankful for what God showed us through Ethan. To date, we have set solid financial goals for our family.

God has blessed us with the ability to give beyond the tithe. We also save 15 percent of our gross income. At any given moment, we know our exact financial position. I no longer worry about car insurance payments! The MAP sets aside a monthly amount for insurance, and I write one check a year. Although I'm still in school, we have already set up a repayment plan for the student loan and it will be paid in full before my grace period ends. No more sleepless nights worrying about money. No more famine, just one great feast. Thanks again, Ethan!"

A Final Note from Ethan

To everyone who wrote these letters, thank you! You have blessed my life, and I am so thankful that God has used the MAP to help you become faithful stewards. I am sure the angels in heaven are applauding you right now.

To everyone who is reading this book, I hope these letters also encouraged you. Did you catch the spirit of what God has done or was doing in these people's lives? Did you sense how using the MAP has relieved stress and frustration? Believe me, if these singles and couples can create a personal money MAP and find success, you can too. *Press on!*

Glossary of Terms

BUDGETOLOGY The theology of using a budget. The Bible frequently addresses the theology of ownership, stewardship, planning, giving, saving, contentment, debt, and wise management of resources. See chapter 4.

COMMISSION INCOME Living on an income that is likely to be different each month because you are being paid a commission on the sales you made last month. These inconsistent paychecks can create many challenges and problems in managing money. See chapter 14.

EMERGENCY FUND Money to help you pay for unexpected expenses that go beyond what you have available in your MAP money box. For example, if you have a $1,000 car repair but you have only $700 in your Car Repair money box, you can use $300 out of your emergency fund to make up the difference. See chapter 6.

FINANCIAL ONENESS God's plan for couples. Couples are to view the resources God has entrusted to them as "our" resources, not "my" resources. Couples should have unified biblical goals, values, and priorities. See chapters 2, 4, and 7.

FIRSTFRUIT GIVING Giving to God first, not last. This demonstrates your faith and trust in God. This demonstrates that God is first in your financial life (see Proverbs 3:9-10). See chapter 6.

GOD OWNS IT ALL The foundational concept in Christian stewardship. All other principles are built on this principle (see Psalm 24:1). See chapter 4.

LIVING BEYOND YOUR MEANS Spending more than you earn. If you consistently spend more than you earn, you will have a financial crisis. Living beyond your means demon-strates a lack of biblical contentment (see Philippians 4:12; 1 Timothy 6:6-8). The only way to live beyond your God-given means is by using debt— which, financially, is very dangerous (see Proverbs 22:7).

MAP Money Allocation Plan (see chapter 5). A simple system to help singles and couples budget money by using one form each month. Three keys to the MAP system are as follows:

1. Based on biblical principles

2. Utilizes predetermined income allocations into money boxes

3. Requires self-control

MAP FORM The actual form you use each month. All you need is one MAP form each month. See chapter 10.

MAP PLANNING WORKSHEET A form you use to help you determine how much monthly income you expect to receive and how much you need to allocate into each of your MAP money boxes. You only need to use this form once to help you create your MAP money boxes and dollar allocations. See chapter 8.

MAP MONEY BOX Term used to communicate a MAP concept. Money for every MAP budget category is put into what I call a money box. It is not a physical box but simply a box on a piece of paper (the MAP form). See chapters 5 and 10.

MAPOLOGY The basic philosophy and concepts for using the MAP. See chapter 5.

MONEY MARKET ACCOUNT Similar to a checking account, but earns interest. It is a safe place to keep money that you might need in the next few days, weeks, or months. See chapter 10.

SIMPLE FINANCIAL PLAN A plan to help you to prioritize your finances. See chapter 6.

STEWARD If God owns it all, we are stewards, or managers, of the resources that God has entrusted to us. Stewards are to be found faithful in the management of God's resources. See chapter 4.

TITHE Giving 10 percent of your income to support God's kingdom. If I earn $1,000 in income, I would give $100 to support God's kingdom. See discussion of giving in chapter 6.

VALUE SYSTEM Everyone spends money based on a series of priorities. Values are reflected every day by what we do, not what we say. Most arguments in a marriage are due to differing values, not the amount of money the couple earns. Values should be biblically based in order to experience true joy and contentment in life. See chapter 7.

ZERO OUT EXPENSES A step in the MAP planning process whereby you mentally reduce all expense categories to zero and then prayerfully evaluate each expense allocation before you record it on your MAP form. Just because you have spent money on something for years does not mean you will continue to spend money (or as much money) on that item in the future. No category is immune from this evaluation step. See chapter 8.

Teaching the MAP to Others

The MAP operates on a simple foundational principle: We cannot take money out of an empty box. No amount of pouting, crying, or scheming can change the fact that a money box is empty. We simply have to wait until another paycheck arrives and more money is allocated into a specific money box. However, if there is money in a box, we have the freedom to leave it in the box or spend it.

Here is a simple yet practical illustration that will help to teach your children about the MAP concept.

Things you will need:
- 5 plastic or foam cups—the throwaway kind
- 5 $1 bills.
- A Magic Marker

The setup:
Take a Magic Marker and write the letter *A* really big on the first cup, the letter *B* on the second cup, the letter *C* on the third cup, the letter *D* on the fourth cup, and the letter *E* on the fifth cup.

Now distribute the dollar bills according to the following MAP plan:
You give the instructions, but have one of your children actually put the money in each cup.

- Place $1 in cup A.
- Place $1 in cup B.
- Place $1 in cup C.

- Place $1 in cup D.
- Place $1 in cup E.

Complete the following instructions:

Once again, as you read the instructions, have one of your children take the money out.

- Take $1 out of cup C.
- Take $1 out of cup A.
- Take $1 out of cup E.
- Take $1 out of cup B.
- Take $1 out of cup A. (The cup is already empty.)

When the child says, "Cup A is empty," reply, "That's right, and it's impossible to take money out of an empty cup, right? The same is true with our family budget. If we decided to put $50 in our Eat Out money box, and all the money is gone, we will not be able to eat out any more this month. It's *impossible* to take something out of nothing."

Endnotes

1. Christine Dugas, "American Seniors Rack Up Debt like Never Before," *USA Today,* April 24, 2002; <www.usatoday.com/money/perfi/retirement/2002-04-25-elderly-debt.htm>.

2. For more information about the side effects of the American societal focus on material gain and growth, visit the Foundations For Living Web site—www.foundationsforliving.org—and click on the "Stat Bank" button.

3. "Mapping Your Stress Points," *Ladies Home Journal,* November 2001, 80.

4. *Merriam-Webster's Collegiate Dictionary,* tenth edition (Springfield, Mass.: Merriam-Webster, Inc., 1993).

5. Ibid.

6. *Webster's New World Dictionary,* second college edition (New York: World Publishing Company, 1970).

7. Ibid.

8. *Merriam-Webster's Collegiate Dictionary.*

9. If you prefer to use a debit card for convenience, it is very important that you establish the habit of recording your expenditures immediately in your checkbook register.

About the Author

ETHAN POPE IS PRESIDENT OF FOUNDATIONS FOR LIVING, A MINISTRY
dedicated to helping people simplify and clarify life issues from
a biblical and practical perspective. He is a graduate of Dallas
Theological Seminary and a CERTIFIED FINANCIAL PLANNER™
certificant, though he does not have a financial planning practice. Ethan is an author, speaker, and regular guest on national
radio programs. His primary field of expertise is the theological and practical aspects of managing money.

Other books by Ethan Pope include *How to Be a Smart Money
Manager; There's No Place Like Home* (with Mary Larmoyeux);
and the *Personal Finance Course.*

Ethan and his wife, Janet, have two teenagers and live in
Hattiesburg, Mississippi.

Foundations For Living

is a ministry dedicated to helping people simplify and clarify life issues
from a biblical and practical perspective.

Mission Statement

Building faithful stewards to manage God's resources, by teaching
foundational truths, primarily through the means of publishing, radio, and speaking,
in order for individuals to experience life to the fullest on earth and in heaven.

For information on:

- Inviting Ethan Pope to speak in your city or church
- Receiving a list of Foundations For Living resources
- Attending a Foundations For Living seminar in your area
- Receiving Foundations For Living publications
- Ordering Foundations For Living's small group study course
- Joining the on-line MAP community on our Web site

Visit our Web site

www.foundationsforliving.org

Write to

Ethan Pope
Foundations For Living
P.O. Box 15356
Hattiesburg, MS 39404

Or call

(601) 582-2000

Order your Start-up MAP Kit:

Receive a discount on your order as our
thank-you for purchasing a copy of this book.

Here's what you will receive:

- One-year supply of 8½″ × 11″ MAP forms
- Sample MAP form
- MAP Planning Worksheets (sample and blank)
- Instructional cassette tape or CD

Be sure to use this special code when placing your order:
TYNMAP

Check out the special MAP area on our Web site for updated MAP information,
MAP Q&A's, MAP money management tips, and MAP user testimonies.